GET EVEN 2:

More Dirty Tricks from the Master of Revenge

GET EVEN 2:

More Dirty Tricks from the Master of Revenge

by George Hayduke

Illustrations by Commander Zero

Paladin Press   Boulder, Colorado

Also by George Hayduke:

Get Even: The Complete Books of Dirty Tricks
Hardcore Hayduke: More Down-and-Dirty Revenge Techniques
The Hayduke Silencer Book
Kickass! More Mayhem from the Master of Malice
Make 'em Pay! Ultimate Revenge Techniques from
    the Master Trickster
Make My Day! Hayduke's Best Revenge Techniques for
    the Punks in Your Life
Payback! Advanced Backstabbing and Mudslinging
    Techniques
Righteous Revenge: Getting Down to Getting Even
Screw Unto Others: Revenge Tactics for All Occasions
Sweet Revenge: A Serious Guide to Retribution
Up Yours! Guide to Advanced Revenge Techniques

Get Even 2: More Dirty Tricks from the Master of Revenge
by George Hayduke

Copyright © 1981 by George Hayduke

ISBN 0-87364-213-9
Printed in the United States of America

Published by Paladin Press, a division of
Paladin Enterprises, Inc., P.O. Box 1307,
Boulder, Colorado 80306, USA.
(303) 443-7250

Direct inquiries and/or orders to the above address.

"There is not much mental distance between a feeling of having been screwed and the ethic of total retaliation, or at least the kind of . . . revenge that comes with outraging the public decency."

—Hunter S. Thompson,
HELL'S ANGELS, 1966.

Contents

Contents

Contents

Introduction

One of the most pleasing compliments I received about the first volume of **Get Even** was from a reader who wrote, "You, George Hayduke, are a hyena in swine's clothing." I cherish that.

Did **Get Even** have an impact? Were the fears of the book distribution company censors justified? Did I get even with the sniggering coward of a radio station manager who cut me off the air during a phone-in talk show in Seattle? Who else got even?

With fascination bordering on glee I noted news reports of creative revenge in towns I visited. Happily, none of the marks were innocent victims. It all seemed to be creative revenge at its most ironic, which is what these books are all about.

Is **Get Even** to blame for social anarchy? Of course not. Just as this book is, the first volume was written solely for entertainment purposes. As one contributor to **Get Even 2** wrote me in his letter, "It's all just in fun, isn't it George." But, should we put a question mark after his rhetorical question?

Even *Playboy* helped out, reporting about the bogus medic nicknamed "Dr. Upchuck" by unamused Miami, Florida victims. It seems a twenty-year-old store clerk had been telephoning female surgery patients at area hospitals, impersonating a staff doctor. He advised these patients to drink many glasses of water, then stick their fingers down their throats enough to regurgitate.

According to the report, as many as 400 patients tossed their cookies because of his sick calls. I checked with one official there who told me the caller made his calls just after mealtimes to add to the spillage decor, no doubt.

Local police described the young man as "sick and having a real problem." But, he explained that his problem was that his girlfriend had been in a local hospital recently when someone called her and upset her so much that she threw up. He just wanted to get even.

I feel the purpose and credo of the first book are even more appropriate now, as the American hand-car to hellish disaster is running out of track. Crooks in power hold our future in their greedy political hands. The San Francisco Bay Area National Lawyers Guild has an official motto which is quite appropriate to the purposes of **Get Even:** "When tyranny is law, revolution is in order."

I was most pleased to read in the daily press that during 1980, telephone companies across the U.S. were being taken by more than $30 million annually by fun folks who charge their calls to random numbers, use fake credit card numbers, or who charge calls to *"the numbers of selected enemies."* I emphasized the latter direct quote from Ma Bell because, in mid-stroke, my ego likes to think that these people who select specific phoney numbers have read **Get Even** and are doing just that with their marks by having long, long, long, and expensive calls charged to the mark's number.

For what it's worth, our peers at American Telephone and Telegraph say that nearly $14 million goes out on fraudulent credit card numbers, which means congratulations are in order to Yippies and to *Overthrow* for their work in getting the good information to the public on how to pirate calls. Also, about $19 million goes to unrelated third party charges. That was one of my suggestions for getting back at your mark. Make a bunch of expensive long distance calls that cannot be traced back to you in any way . . . and charge them to your mark's number.

Interestingly, in their report, AT & T said their figures do not include the additional millions paid by innocent subscribers who never check the long distance calls on their bills and simply pay them without realizing they are being charged for someone else's call.

Another reader sent in a cautionary motto that would be well to follow as you join us in this new battleground of creative revenge. He suggests "Be an opportunist—not a daredevil." That's because, sometimes the machines and their masters fight back. An article from the *Cincinnati Enquirer* described how a young man was especially bothered by an automated, afterhours money-dispensing machine at his local bank. You put in your card, things click and you get your cash. Robert Wenger didn't get his cash, though. So, he punched the machine, and his blow knocked it out of commission. Yet, the machine retained Wenger's name in its memory as the last transaction before having its lights punched out.

After the police, the courts came next. Paying his $857 in damages and fines, Wenger said, "I was upset, but I didn't mean to break it."

Score one for the computers. But, let's not let that one go unanswered, please.

Working on this book I noted that the current scams are not as light or as humorous as the first volume. I didn't laugh as often. But, as nearly two-thirds of this book are ideas sent in by readers of the first volume I guess that people are a lot more frustrated than even I believed. That frightens me.

Some of the stuff in here is very nasty. But, don't lose your sense of humor, please! Remember, whether or not you use the contents of this book actively, keep your sense of humor. Please note that in both books, most of the marks don't have any sort of sense of humor. It is vital that you do.

As with the first book, there are many ideas, tricks, marks and scams that could be cross referenced. For example, in this volume, there's a stunt involving beer, urine and apple juice that could involve a total cross reference of a dozen types of marks and a dozen other scams. So, don't restrict your planning to one category or chapter. Let your nasty fingers creep through the entire book. Or, as those cliche-mongering TV baseball announcers say, "A good player doesn't just play the ball, he uses the whole field."

Get Even 2 is truly the product of your cards and letters sharing your favorite rotten stunts performed in the name of do-it-yourself justice. Seeing my manuscript for the first time, my friend and publisher Peder Lund shook his head and sighed that this was truly an indicative barometer of the disastrous state of our society. Despite Peder's sensitivities, I would like to issue another invitation for all readers, repeat and first timers alike, to send me many more stunts, scams, tricks, and ideas, so we can build a third volume. In the meantime, happy reading, tricking and treating.

Additives

For those who have graduated from the gum-on-the-seat-of-the-pants school, here's a suggestion from a friendly basement chemist. Pour a small amount of low molarity acid on a wooden or hard plastic chair seat. If your mark doesn't notice the moisture and sits in it, his or her clothing will melt in moments, exposing the mark's posterior for some of the world to see. It's a cheeky way to get back at your mark, perhaps for humiliating you some way in public. Why not make an ass out of someone you loathe today?

Shopping in Mother Nature's pharmacy is a delight for the trickster. That hale world wanderer, Col. Martin Nelson Chunder, favors toxin from *Bufo americanus* and *Bufo vulgaris*, the common toad so maligned in tale and fable.

"Many toads secrete a substance which varies from poisonous to irritating," Col. Chunder reports. "A good chemist can supply you with the toad toxin of your liking. You have merely to apply it to your mark, your mark's food or whatever you choose. The result will be most uncomfortable to the mark, but rewarding for you."

He advocates care, though, as some of these toad substance additives can be quite toxic.

Here's a second batch of fine additive ideas from our good friend, Dr. Edward Watson. Rather than get into specific cases or instances as I have done in other sections of this book, I will let our malicious medico deliver his own pharmacological lecture.

"If used correctly, pharmacology can be a formidable weapon in one's arsenal. The drug LARGACTYL is an especially effective "knockout" drug, and works well in coffee, tea and other beverages. Simply grind two tablets into powder and put into the mark's beverage. In 20 to 30 minutes the mark will be counting sheep."

This was a favorite ploy of the bar girls in Saigon, when hustling new GI's just off the plane, I might add.

The Dr. continues, "PURIDIUM is a drug which, if introduced into a mark's coffee or other beverage, will result in him urinating in shades from dark brown to bright orange. That's great for making your mark think he or she has some sort of exotic social disease or serious medical ailment. There's no pain or aftereffect, but this will scare hell out of the mark.

"Get some plaster packs, you know, the kind doctors use for casts. These are readily available at orthopedic supply houses or you can steal some from a local hospital or clinic. The trick is to get the mark drunk or otherwise indisposed and then apply the casts (they require only soaking in warm water and are quick drying). One's imagination is the only limit to the kind of tricks that can be played with this stuff.

"Another effective 'sleep' drug is MOGADON, which is relatively new on the market. It's powerful

2

stuff, and a small amount is more than enough to zonk out the average person. Use it with caution, but use it well."

A bit of hirsute handicapping came in from Wilbur Aaron, who writes that Wesson oil makes a great substitute for any of the golden colored hair conditioners. He reports of one case in which it was several days before the mark noticed something was seriously amiss, as in a bad case of the greasies.

John's wife and one of her girlfriends used to go out a couple nights of the week seeking a dose of recreational sex after some alcohol-fueled disco action. She wasn't especially concerned about John's feelings. Instead of shooting someone, though, John got some Nyquil and started adding heavy doses of this drug to the anticipatory drinks wifey had at home before her girlfriend picked her up for their carnal cruising. John says the "medicine" struck about 10 pm and his wife would literally fall asleep at the table in the disco, never making it to the motel time segment of the evening.

John says that a couple times he slipped enough of the stuff into her pre-dinner cocktails so she was at home and sound asleep by 8 pm.

Chuckling the laugh of the satisfied, John adds, "Then, I went out looking for some action. Why should I suffer all the cuckolding?"

For those moralists who are shaking in indignant outrage, this marriage, which was bonded only in bourbon and Nyquil, soon dissolved.

You can easily modify this approach to do in someone who needed to get a good night's sleep.

One reader suggested using something like No Doz with the mark's evening meal, especially if that person needs to get a great sleep for some important function the next day. Usually, the mark will never figure out why he or she is staring at a dark ceiling at 2 am instead of being blissfully asleep.

Airlines

On his flight out from Atlanta, Maj. Bezallel Howe was overbooked on a popular airline. He had a hard time claiming the bumping money due him by law. He reports the "wings of man" people were quite rude. He finally got a flight out three hours later. A week later, on his return flight, he was bumped again. His next flight ticket was screwed up. This took place in St. Louis, where they were at least semi-friendly, Maj. Howe reports.

Finally, back in Atlanta and ready to go out again, the Major found his flight was to be delayed two hours for mechanical reasons. He fumed, then while sitting in an airport lemonade lounge watching a baseball game on tv, he was further infuriated when he saw a sweetsy commercial for his "favorite" airline.

"My next stop was the custom t-shirt shop in the airport mall area. It took a bit of bartering, but I finally got them to make me a shirt with this legend on the front—EASTERN AIRLINES EATS SHIT," Maj. Howe says.

Wearing his new t-shirt, he then paraded back and forth in the Eastern Airlines ticket area of the Atlanta airport. Several people came up to congratulate him and to share their own woes, and instead of arresting him, a security guard offered to buy him a drink. We were unable to get Frank Borman's response to this revenge.

Air Conditioner

In the interest of saving energy and being less self-indulgent, I am passing along this idea from Wilbur Aaron's brother. He says you can sabotage a window-mounted air conditioner with nothing more than a wad of chewing gum. The rationale for this is up to you, of course. I hope only that it's justified. Anyway, you simply stuff that wad of Wrigley's Best up the condensation drain tube of the unit. With luck your mark won't notice the overflow until his floor tiles lift off from the flooding moisture.

Animals

Back in the late '70s, Philadelphia was entertained by a bunch of ugly, off the wall anarchists who called themselves MOVE. One of the tamer things these anti-social dingoes did was breed and raise large, nasty wharf rats which they used to annoy their enemies, i.e., anyone but themselves. A dirty trickster could pair large nasty rats, then release their healthy offspring near or in the mark's home or place of business. Be sure to leave adequate feed at the target area for the rats so they'll feel welcome. Come back every few evenings and leave more feed for them. You can pretend you're the animal world's welcome wagon, and your rats will have your mark by the tail.

For some reason those gross, ugly Philadelphia ghetto rats remind me of the personality of that city's 1980 World Series baseball team. But, if spreading that kind of critter and his fear around isn't to your style, you could simply use his tame, clean cousin, the relatively vapid laboratory rat sold in pet shops and medical supply stores.

My friend Devon from Colorado says that America suffers from Ratphobia, as books and films have profitably documented. He says dirty tricksters can

take advantage of this without slumming around with the real thing. Here's his suggestion.

"Go to your local pet shop or lab supply house and buy a few of those big 'tame' rats they sell. Go for large brown ones. The vast majority of people wouldn't know the difference between a wild and tame rat."

He's right. I don't. Do you?

Devon says they cost between $2 and $3 each. His plan is to place two or three in a sack that is loosely rolled shut. Place the sack under your target's desk, sofa, bed, carseat, office, or hospital room, then leave the area.

Openly laughing now, Devons says, "The rats will work their way out of the sack in moments. I promise you, this is guaranteed to scare the living (crudity deleted) out of all the folks present. You can be sure hysteria will quickly take hold in the area. With luck, much time and money will be spent with some local exterminator to get rid of these 'wild, dirty, vicious pests."

This next scene is something each person who has ever been hurt by a lover will feel. You know the protagonist of this episode because it could have been you. Enough literary maudlinism, it's time to get tough here. The young lady's married lover cheated on her, as well as his wife, beat her up, sexually abused her and tried to turn her apartment into a brothel for himself and his friends while she was at work. He was a real rat.

Our lady friend asked a friend of her brother to help her get even with the rat. Our friend's friend, armed with a display case full of product samples called on the home of the Rat. Mrs. Rat, who really wasn't a bad sort, but, guilt by marriage is probable cause, was at home and welcomed the young "salesman."

While sitting on the expensive new sofa, our "salesman" diverted Mrs. Rat's attention with his products. While she was literally looking the other way, he carefully reached into his coat pocket and brought forth a handful of baby mice, placing them in the underparts of the sofa to nurture and grow. He thought quietly, 'Go forth and multiply, little ones.'

On his way out the door, the salesman could not resist saying "Have a Mice Day," which Mrs. Rat misheard as something else.

OK, so this next one is only a fraternity trick. If you're so damned smart, then you improvise, modify or adopt this basic idea to something more insidious. Here's what happened originally.

At an unidentified college in Colorado, members of Kappa Sigma fraternity purchased an elk's head and two sheep's heads from a local taxidermist and set them on the sun deck of their frat house to ripen. When the heads had rotted and were covered with maggots, the Kappa Sigs went to the Phi Delta house, planted the elk's head in the living room, and stuffed the sheep's heads down the chimney.

Is the man from Orkin still laughing? I am.

What's the matter? Is the neighbor's dog pooping up your property or yellowing your lawn? Read on. You can discourage dogs from coming around your place if you feed them, using an additive, of course. Insert a crystal of menthol or some smelling salts in a chunk of meat, a doggie candy or some other treat the offensive brute will enjoy. When the goody melts down to the additive, the bite will outdo

12

the bark. If your world's not going to the dogs, how about the howl of the wild.

Ask any farmer how he feels about wild critters in his corn field. Deer not only eat it, they stomp down the plants. A groundhog or raccoon can decimate a peck of ripe sweet corn in an evening. Are any clever ideas beginning to form in your mind, gentle reader? Pat Homer was infuriated when some two-legged wild critters ruined her cornfield. These critters were strip miners whose refuse overflow tumbled downhill, landing in destructive heaps upon Homer's sweetcorn. "Breaks of the game . . . sue us," they told Pat Homer.

Not only did Pat Homer take them to court, she also found out that the wealthy boss strip miner lived on a pleasant little estate not far away. The estate featured a sweet corn plot of which Mr. Strip Mine Land Rapist was most proud. The corn had been developed for him by the state university in exchange for promise of a large cash donation.

After doing her intelligence analysis, Pat Homer went to a nearby gun shop and bought some Scrape Mate, the trade name of a triple-strength game lure. The scene is Doe in Heat. Guess what that will attract if spread liberally over Mr. Land Rapist's cornfield?

Pat told me, "I'm a great believer in that stuff. It works. The clerk told me only a few drops will attract herds of deer from great distances. Think what the whole bottle did. Every deer in the state was in that bastard's garden that night and the next night. They wiped out his crop better than he'd done to mine with his draglines."

An ear for an ear, I always say.

Even though a rubber snake is supposed to be a funny gag, tell that to someone who's just been bitten or frightened by the real thing. For some reason, snakes are guaranteed adrenalin pumpers for most of us. Obviously, this means a grand potential for dirty tricks, which brings to mind Synanon and their infamous add-a-rattlesnake to the mailbox trick. That's a bit out of our league, not to mention being out of someone else's mind.

The same basic scenario can be used, though, by substituting a rubber snake. As luck would have it, Johnson Smith (see SOURCES) sells a very realistic looking rubber snake. So do many hobby shops. Look around until you find something slimey and yukky enough to make even a toughie like you get squeamish. Buy several and use them as your imagination and evil sense of creative revenge see fit. In addition to mailboxes, the bogus snakes could be introduced under beds, chairs, in sleeping bags, boots, tool boxes, under car seats, on clothes or linen closets about eye height. Or, place them in the mark's basement or garage. The location are limitless. I do hope your mark has a strong heart, though. Seriously!

Apartment

Here's a switch, a landlord seeking revenge against tenants. Rob Roosel claimed that the hippies he rented to were tearing up his place. He tried the entire law book of legal ways to get back, all without success. So, he waited until he finally had these obnoxious tenants exterminated from his place by virtue of the lease expiring. He made very sure he knew where the tribe had moved. Happily, they bought a small house of their own in another neighborhood. Roosel smiled.

He explained, "I got a few yards of rubber tubing from a science supply store, attached it to a large funnel, drank about 27 beers, then visited their Hippie Heaven. I slipped the tubing under their door and offloaded all that beer-fed urine into the funnel. I did that every night for four days. When I came back on the fifth night I noted they had put in a porch light and had a 'Beware of Dog' sign in the yard."

Roosel added, "Hee Hee Hee."

If you don't like beer 'n urine, then hold the onions for your mark's abode. That is, you can bury onions inside flowerpots, particularly those near heaters or radiators in the wintertime. The stench soon becomes overpowering, but is unlocatable.

15

John P. Neal offers another suggestion for the new miracle glues as a household weapon. He had a landlord who was an absolute waste when it came to doing anything about the lack of heat in the apartment. John was freezing. After getting nowhere on his last complaint, John gave notice and was moving out. When he went to the landlord's home to get back his security deposit, he had a friend, by prearranged time signal, call the landlord on the telephone—in another room. Quickly, John went to the landlord's thermostat, turned it to its maximum, then used quick drying Super-Glue to lock the controls at that setting. He also put glue on the screws which gave access to the instrument. Finally, he put a glue seal around the device and the wall. He heard that the landlord had to use a wrecking bar to pry the thermostat off the wall and a furnace man had to come in to put things right.

The landlord tried to sue John, but had no proof. He should have known better. If justice really worked, we wouldn't need books like this, would we?

Old time trapper Zeb Porkmore got stung by a fast talking salesman who ripped him off by leasing him a horrible apartment. Zeb tracked the real estate scoundrel to his own place. Then, he did his intelligence gathering homework. He tells the rest of his story.

"You know about those liquid room fresheners that come in small bottles? I have the reverse of that in mind. I got a one ounce bottle of animal trapping lure. Some of these lures are the ugliest smelling crap known in the civilized world. Most are made of ground up unmentionable glands mixed in with

16

some of the dead animal's urine. The whole mess is allowed to putrify. Only a few drops will attract other animals to traps or whatever.

"What is wonderful is that only a few drops are also enough to turn the stomach of even the most case-hardened mortician. A few drops of any of these lures in your mark's apartment will instantly sicken your target. There is no known way to get rid of the stink for a few days."

I also figured the same stuff would work in a car, an elevator, a conference room, a courtroom or on the mark's clothing. On second thought, why not use it on the mark himself? If your mark behaves like an uncivilized animal, then he or she should smell like one, too.

A refinement to the exploding apartment light fixture I explained in the first book, whereby you tape a bag of fresh feces loaded with an explosive charge and wired to the mark's light switch in his or her room, came from Chris Loop. He suggests you substitute a payload of fresh worms, small dead animals, raw sewage, vomit, paint, urine, or a combination of any of the above.

Athletics

Veteran Major League pitcher Tug McGraw confounded Bowie Kuhn and the other pompous poops of the baseball establishment when he advised young fans, "Always root for the winner, and you'll avoid disappointment." For that wisdom, we award Tug the Bill Lee Bovine Effluvia Award with Corn Flake Cluster.

All ex-jocks recall the legendary effects of a dose of analgesic balm in someone else's jockstrap cup. Perhaps even some of you victims are still soaking in cold water these many years later. Technology and better living through chemistry now offer a better burn without the greasy, easily smelled mess of the balm.

According to famed supporter Sharon Bendover, a dose of Sea Breeze in your mark's jock pocket will do the same, only better, than the old balm trick. But, if you are going to use the old fashioned greasy kid stuff, why not try one of the newer brands on the market, especially that atomic rocket goody that big league pitchers use to crockpot their arms. Have a ball!

Automobiles

What do you get when you mix windshield washer and paint remover? The answer is, not nearly as much as the new "miracle" paint remover used all by itself, as we'll see. One gentle reader finally tired of being called "queer, fag, homo" because he was a quiet loner who liked books better than boobs. His tormentors were the typical Main Street camheads who cruise your town too. Although he calls them "low riders," he did far worse to them.

"They park their cars all over town, but never lock them. I simply got under the hood, drained the windshield washer bottle, and replaced that solution with that new 'miracle' paint remover. Wow . . . what results. It's a great way to ruin a paint job."

My pal Bob from Southern California delights in doing dirty to the automobiles of his marks. While living in a rented house, Bob found that the house drains worked more like fountains than waste disposal devices. He complained to his uncaring landlord who ignored the situation, forcing Bob to fix the drains himself, stew awhile, then get even.

"How about pouring Draino into my mark's car radiator?" Bob reports. "I had to use Draino to alleviate my suffering, so I decided to use it to further his."

Draino eats out the copper tubing and will eventually destroy the entire cooling system of the vehicle.

Some of Bob's other anti-car actions include putting several drops of skunk oil, available from many sporting goods outlets, on sparkplug recess areas. This is undetectable until the vehicle's occupants notice the horrible odor that lingers and lingers and lingers. It also stays with the clothing of your mark and his/her friends, too.

He also suggests taking powder from a road fuse and place it into the cigarette lighter recepticle. When the mark pushes in the lighter button, the powder ignites, causing a bit of a flash, followed by the acrid stench of sulfur fumes.

A friendly Canadian reader, Ron Lank, has a passion for automobile tricks. He reports that as a high schooler, he had a friend who had been attacked with M80 firecrackers. To get back at his attacker, the friend got a piece of bicycle innertube and fastened it to the tailpipe of his mark's car. It was held in place with a radiator hose clamp.

The mark started the car and roared off. Within moments, there was a horrible sound from the back of the car. Screeching to a stop, the car bucked as the mark bailed out. His face turned scarlet as he spotted the length of innertube. He was furious and grabbed the tube to yank it off. He should not have done that, because the engine was still idling. Exhaust gases were still coming into the tube. When he grabbed the tube, his fist prevented the gases from escaping from the open end of the tube. It exploded in the kid's face. He was physically unhurt, but his pants were somewhat stained.

Daniel Jacson used this one during the gasoline shortages of the late '70s, when people used to cut into gas station lines and do other rude, selfish things to get fuel. Wearing a uniform like service station workers use, he would stroll up to offending vehicles and tell them he was preparing them for service. He removed their normal gas caps and replaced them with locking caps. He then walked far away and changed clothes.

Daniel says this trick, while expensive, is great fun. He says you can also do this anytime you locate your mark's vehicle alone and unattended, even if it's not in a gas line. With luck the mark will never notice until it's too late.

Here's one the mark will notice. You're trying to park your family chariot close in at the shopping center lot and you see what looks like an open space. You nose in, only to face some hoopy's car parked across the dividing line, sitting two feet into your space.

Or, you park further down, and some hillbilly with his knucles dragging on the ground will throw open his junker's door and bash hell out of your car's finish.

Or, you go through the same exercise a couple isles over and find some pointy-head idiot has stuck his Lincoln Continental in the middle of three spaces—to save his baby from being scratched by the slamming of some common economy car.

Johnny Johnson has a wonderful solution.

"I'm simply furious when I encounter such a thing. I'm a chartered accountant and I like things neat—even parking. Here's what I do.

"I keep my keys in my hand when I park my car—away from these offenders. Then, I project the toughest, longest key I have as I walk toward the rudely parked cars. As I walk by that big Detroit Mastodon, I simply rip the tip of my key alongside the body of that car.

"I advise you to check first to be certain the cretin who owns that car is not in it at this time. Also, check for other witnesses.

"With the proper angle and a little pressure I can inflict a ⅛ inch deep rip the entire length of the vehicle. When I come back from the store, if the car is still there, I do the other side."

I would add one bit of warning to Johnny Johnston's highly illegal plan. I advise against the second attack. The mark may have discovered the initial hit and could be waiting for your second move. I would cool it after one pass.

I used to live in a town with far more than its share of automotive slobs. These include the slimeballs who park along the No Parking curbside zones at shopping malls; who park in spots reserved for handicapped folks; who double-park while their 800 pound spouse and swarm of demented offspring unpile from the vehicle. Sometimes these inconsiderate imbeciles park in the area that you rent to park your own car. Or, they will park in a doctor's office lot, or in a small shop's lot, or in front of your home, or in your slot in the apartment lot, etc. In that town I lived in, the local gestapo were too busy using their police dogs to terrorize college students to bother

with slob parking violators. The local merchants cringed at the idea of insulting potential customers so they refused to even protest the horrid conditions caused by illegal and inconsiderate parking.

Maybe you're a kindly soul who can't bring yourself to dragging a key across their car. If so, it's Johnson Smith to the rescue of your sensitive feelings (see SOURCES). Johnson Smith is a mail order trickster's shop. Among other items they sell a pad of pre-printed yellow forms that look exactly like municipal parking tickets. The Johnson Smith tickets contain PG-rated insults about the lack of parking ability and consideration of the "simple minded driver." You simply fill in the normal parking ticket data like a real cop, then stick the insulting bogus ticket on the offender's windshield, under the wiper blade.

As a modification of this idea, you can get your own tickets custom-printed. Your tickets should say far worse things about the slob driver, his mother, and other people and ideas he or she might hold sacred. Yours can be either R or X rated. I will leave that to your own selective sense of humor and frustration. Yes, I know these tame tickets aren't as much fun as using epoxy to glue whole sheets of newsprint over the slob's windshield, or spray painting the windshield, or even spraying it with birdshot, from a shotgun. But, I feel I must include some revenge for the more gentle souls among us, too. Cough.

Even people from New York enjoyed **Get Even.** Two of them calling themselves Peter Brown and his friend Fat Man offers a nuts 'n bolts way of shutting down the headlights of your mark's car in a rather violent way.

You need to have some M60s. These are the scaled down, sissy version replacing the famed M80. But, however tame, they will do the job, but not as well as with as much BARROOM. Anyhow, you also need to get to a nearby hobby shop and buy some igniters for the "jet" engines of the playground missiles. You will also need wirecutters, bell wire, electrical tape, and a screwdriver.

Tape two thin bellwires to the igniter wires. Tape well. Remove the headlights from your mark's car. I assume you will do this at an appropriate time or place after a careful intelligence analysis. Then, tape the igniter fuse to the fuse of the M60. Twist the other igniter wire to the wire that was hooked to the headlight. Stick the firecracker and the wiring back into the light headlight cavity, then replace the light. Guess what happens when your mark turns on his headlight switch?

As these guys note, "Boy do I feel sorry not only for the mark but for anything in front of him when the M60s let go behind those headlights. It's great."

That reminds me of a poor man's Claymore mine. Anyway, the guys say that not only are M60s easy to come by in New York, but that you can still get M80s easily. I'd love to know how. My own supply is almost gone.

There are myriad of reasons to get back at your mark via his automobile. To that point, a correspondent claiming to be the Master Mechanic, got Haydukian ideas while drunk and wrote me with some splendid advice. With all due deference I present his ideas in succinct order.

• Remove the coil terminal (the middle one) from the distributor. Dampen a piece of cigarette rolling paper and cram it as far down in the coil tower as it will go. The mark's car might chug about five miles before rolling to a mysterious stop. My man claims most utility grade mechanics, e.g., about 85 percent of them, will miss spotting this trick. That keeps your mark's car tied up in the garage for more hours and dollars.

• A very, very *small* amount of solvent in the master cylinder of a brake system will slowly eat away all rubber parts, causing a gradual and expensive breakdown of the brake system.

• Using a very fine grindstone, place a very tiny hole in the glass of a parking light bulb. Do this near the metallic base. Fill this hole with black powder. Replace this "bomb." If all works well, the explosive force will not only shatter the parking light lens, but will also provide a splendid display of fireworks.

• Placing salt in the mark's auto radiator is a long term scam for delayed gratification. Our Master Mechanic friend suggests a pound will move things along the trail to decay much faster.

• In addition to other paint remover, brake fluid spilled on a car's painted surface will give the vehicle a sloppy, unwanted two-tone paint job.

• The steering wheels of some of today's fancy cars (read excessively expensive) have an emblem cover over the steering wheel column, hiding the retaining bolt. His idea is pry off the emblem, remove the bolt totally, then replace the emblem. Result: "Look ma, no hands. . . ."

• Don't forget additives in the transmission, mixed right in with those fancy fluids "they" tell you to put in there. I am currently experimenting with pouring styrene in my mark's transmission fluid reservoir. More later on this.

That's it from our own resident Master Mechanic, who prefers the initials M.M. and who says he will refine what he has, experiment with more, then give me the proven results for the third volume of getting back at the bad guys and girls.

This isn't really funny, and smacks of pure camhead hooliganism, but Wilbur Aaron says it wasn't especially humorous, either, when some rodders tried to run his brother off the road. Wilbur says he gave them a bit of a driving lesson in return.

"One dark night I carefully removed one of the U-joints from the drive shaft of their car and loosened the nuts holding the bolts on the second joint. Somewhere between home and school the rodder's car dropped its drive shaft right down there on the road," Wilbur noted.

He also suggests another disabling auto scam in which you loosen the drain plug on the engine oil pan. You leave it 2 or 3 turns short of falling out, so that the normal bumps and bounces of pothole driving will drop the plug and allow the oil to flee the engine. Wilbur says this one's a sure burn out number.

Aaron suggests another additive for the mark's automobile engine, saying, "This one won't be found on the shelf of your local discount store along with 6020 other auto products and additives. You get this from your neighborhood sandbox."

Yes, he's suggesting that old standby of putting sand in the crank-case of the mark's motorcar. Enough sand will clog the oil filter so that the now-gritty lubricant will bypass the filter and rumble through the engine, destroying piston rings and bearings. Soon, the expensive, once powerful engine will be suitable only for use as a boat anchor, large door stop or primitive sculpture.

Bars

This is just a little harmless fun. If your neighborhood bar has funny, visual signs of MEN and WOMEN on or above the restroom doors perhaps you could dream up a funny sign to go with TRANSVESTITES, which you could then place on a door nearby, like the kitchen, office, closet, etc.

Bathrooms

There once was a young reader from Maryland who told me he was the son of a professional sniper. Beyond that, he doesn't want his name in print as he shares some bathroom banter with you. He suggests that a quart of turpentine flushed down a commode will cause a rupture of that facility's plumbing. I checked this with a friend who is a plumber and he just laughed. I called a former housing contractor who had been a premier juvenile delinquent in our youth. He didn't know anything about this stunt. We have not tried this and must warn the reader about possible dangerous consequences.

Bathtubs

Just because a lot of good clean fun can happen in a bathtub if the right people are present doesn't mean dirty work can't be applied. Boswell G. Pendleton suggests that if you want to really roast your mark, you either place a copious amount—like two jars—of commercial meat tenderizer in his or her bathwater, or have an accomplice do it. According to Pendleton, it's much more fun if you can have a liberal-minded assistant do it, because of the entire scenario of social intercourse, dining foreplay, coy sparring, etc., etc., culminating in a "rich soaking bath" before the main event.

"It works well on any of the three sexes," Pendelton advises. "And, the surprise is wonderful. The best part is that the jerk in the tub actually starts to cook as the tenderizer is a hell of an irritant. The discomfort alone is a totally adequate excuse to discontinue the evening. I heartily recommend this one."

From an expert like that, the endorsement stands on its own.

Moving up from the tub to the shower head, I saw a potentially good idea in the Goldie Hawn comedy film *Private Benjamin*. It involved getting back at a mark by packing the pipe or cavity behind the shower head with a concentrated solution of brightly colored dye. The mark hits the shower, hopefully with eyes shut, the water filters through the dye and hopefully transfers to the mark. It worked well in the film, which is, of course, par for Hollywood.

In your interest I asked several domestic experts if this trick had any basis in reality. All said it did, but not to the dramatic extent of success in the film. But, all said it would work to varying degrees depending upon the amount and concentration of dye, color of dye, permanency of the solution, amount of time between placement and shower use, temperature and pressure of the water, etc. But, all did agree the basic plan would work. They suggested experimentation. I thought that sounded like a peachy keen idea, too. Maybe it's time you put your favorite showertime mark on a dyette.

Booze

As every dedicated alcholic knows, the prescription drug "Antabuse" which is really Disulfiram will make a person dreadfully ill if taken with booze. The drug is prescribed for recovering alcholics to insure that if they do slip off the wagon and take a drink, they will get sick as can be if they are also taking their Antabuse medication.

The reader who suggested this idea cautions that you should not mix the drug directly with alcohol. Get the drug into the mark some other way, prior to the ingestion of alcohol. The reader says the drug is not all that tough to get, despite being a prescription item. But, it is much more potent than the Ipecac mentioned in our first volume. Be careful.

For some mysterious reason a number of my friends are truly hardcore beer drinkers. You know, the kind of guys who think an after dinner speech is a horrendous belch . . . ? Anyway, Norman Althree and his roommate Cricket Easter had these really bad neighbors who used to wander over, uninvited, and rip off pitcher after pitcher of draft beer during parties hosted by my friends. These freeloading swine never offered to even up, barter, or make any hospitable gesture.

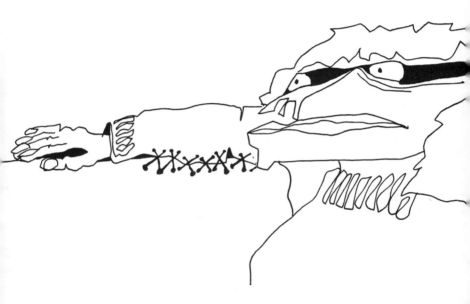

Naturally, some gesture was in order by some-one.

At the next soiree, when the cheapies showed up for their fifth refill, Norman had a special pitcher for them. By this time, the nefarious neighbors were enough sheets to the wind that they were hogging down anything that looked like beer.

Urine looks a lot like beer, especially when it's fresh and has a good head on it. Mixing in a little beer can complete the disguise, Norman says.

Norman passed along another version in which beer that is four or five days stale and flat can be put into commercial apple juice bottles and distributed. He says, "You can give them to people like our now ex-neighbors or you sneak the bogus juice into their refrigerators. I guess you could use this same idea if you got angry enough at a supermarket.

"Just load up a few apple juice bottles with one of your substitutes and place it back on the shelf. Security people look for you sneaking food out of a store, but who looks for you sneaking it in!"

He makes a point. Apple cider anyone?

Sheree West is a delightful mistress of mayhem whose good looks and petite appearance totally disguise her tough, rottenly evil sense of revenge. A lover of animals, she has been known to introduce mice and/or sparrows to the homey environment of her mark's automobile upholstery or the mark's home. She says, too, that mealworms may be dropped in cereal boxes, etc.

Her hallmark to date, though, involved a besot-ted roommate who would stumble in obnoxiously drunk night after night, spilling all her life's sob-sister tragedies, as well as her evening's food and drink, all over the apartment.

Enough! Sheree waited until an especially bad evening. She had personally seen her roommate inhale the contents of seven beers as her final consumption of that evening, then fall into her usual passout supine position in bed, all without visiting the bathroom to offload the used beer by-product.

Our lovely little nastiness carefully and deftly sewed her blottoed buddy's clothes shut, including the fly buttons on her pants. Sheree sewed her roommate's long blouse sleeves to her pants legs. Then, she sewed Dolly Drunk's blouse, slacks and socks to the bed. Finally, she placed the sad souse's hand in a bowl of warm water.

The mark started to get that desperate urge to answer nature's call and sort of woke up. But, she couldn't get mobile enough to leave her bed, no matter how hard she struggled. You can guess the rest, i.e., to reissue the coinage of Women's Lib slogan, "You can sleep in the wet spot tonight" when you're the mark and your fate is all sewed up.

Bumper Stickers

A simple refinement was suggested to permantize unwanted bumper stickers that you place on your mark's auto. Be sure to use one of the new, modern glues over and under to insure the sticker will not be easily removed. That's gentle, compared to the next paragraph.

Although no sane person would literally endorse this idea, it's a hell of an attention getter, especially in a center city area. This time the message on your bumper sticker is a terse, KILL POLICE. Or, if you're squeamish, use MAIM POLICE. You get the idea. The one time I know of this being used was when someone placed it on the bumper of a city councilman who was a stoneage era redneck with an IQ of just about room temperature. It upset his buddies at the cop house badly and they never quite trusted that councilman again. An unforgiving hippie waited a long time to get his partial revenge on that politician.

Butane Lighters

Early in 1980, the American news media sensationalized rumors of the horrible dangers of butane lighters. With their usual lack of checking for accuracy, they printed wild stories about accidental deaths caused by butane lighters exploding with the power of three sticks of dynamite. Sensing this to be nonsense, I contacted OSHA, The National Safety Council, and several other organizations to verify the claims. They turned out to be totally untrue.

However, butane lighters will explode if exposed to sparks, fire, or intense heat. One nasty type who used to do contract work for the CIA suggested, jokingly, of course, that a butane lighter be shoved into the tailpipe of your mark's car, then moved along with a stiff wire until it drops into the muffler. The heat will explode the butane lighter, he claims.

Perhaps it would be well to test this on an abandoned car before it is really put to the test under field conditions. If this suggestion bothers more sensitive readers, then simply turn the premise to the negative, i.e., don't shove butane lighters into automobile mufflers.

Camping

One of Canada's prime tricksters is also a camping aficionado. But, as Ron Lank likes his privacy and peace undisturbed, he sometimes runs into unruly campers who don't follow this golden rule of the wilds. Ron has developed some ways for dealing with crude and rude campers.

Ron says that empty bug repellant bottles can be washed out thoroughly and the contents be refilled with something sweet like pancake syrup or sugar water . . . sure to draw insects. The bogus juice is then left in the mark's campsite where it will be used.

"This stuff works well at night when the drunks just see the label and slap the stuff on. Sometimes, so many mosquitos show up the poor mark is tempted to give up camping forever. But, no such luck, the bad ones seldom do," Ron reports.

Another Lank trick is to get into conversation with the rude campers, then bring up the "snake problem" at that campsite. Tell the mark that the snakes aren't really a problem because they come out only at night when everyone is inside his camper or tent, all zipped up and snakeproof.

"Besides, I don't believe that rumor about three

people being bitten by snakes this past week. At least nobody died, anyway!

"You might also ask the mark if he has a snake-bite kit. Tell him he should maybe have two of them—just in case."

Ron once camped next to a group that had a loud, non-stop party all night. The following day, while the revelers slept, Ron scouted up a nearby poison ivy patch, then quietly swiped all the firewood from the drunkards' campsite. He put a few sticks in the poison ivy patch. When they started their party up again at dusk, the drunks saw Ron's nice camp fire. Drunkenly missing their own wood and thinking they had burned it all the night before, they asked "Good Neighbor Ron" where he got his wood. Remember that poison ivy patch, gentle reader?

That's exactly where Ron sent them to gather firewood, knowing they'd not see the noxious weed at night. Ron was up and gone the following morning so he missed their itchy agony. However, before leaving he noted with a grin that the poison ivy patch had been thoroughly trampled and much of it had been uprooted by hand and tossed around as the drunks tore through there looking for firewood. There are other suggestions.

If your mark is camping in bear country, be sure to rub ground beef all over the roof of his/her car at night. Mix in some honey, too. Big, hungry bears will climb up on the hood and roof of the vehicle to get at the goodies. Hopefully, they will dent it, cave it in, and, at the very least, scratch it badly. If you do the same thing to the Mark's tent or camper, the bears might ruin that. This could be dangerous, because

the bruins might destroy the mark, also. But, nobody ever said camping was easy.

Another favorite on the bruin menu is sardine oil. It is the best lure for bears, according to my hunter friends. You simply spray the sardine oil or pour it over your mark's equipment or vehicle. I've always thought bears were really neat animals. Now I know they are.

Another camping funbit comes from Jacques Beel. Again, rowdy folks who don't know enough to observe the quiet hours became the marks after an evening of keeping decent folks awake. The four bad guys had a large tent with an attached floor. This structure was their environmental envelope, as things turned out.

About 6 a.m., just as the sun was peeking a sleepy eye open over the hills, a 4 x 4 Jeep coasted to a stop beside the offenders' tent. Quietly, a person got out and hooked a rope from the vehicle's trailer hitch on the eight guying grommets on the tent. A few seconds later the Jeep spun out, dragging the lumpy, noisy envelope through a rough meadow at the edge of the campground, through a stream, roaring into the mucky edge of the nearby lake, then doing a high speed turn while the passenger in the Jeep cut the towing rope at the apex of the turn. Guided by that great law of physics, the tentful of marks tumbled end over battered end into four feet of water. Beel's vehicle roared off . . . unknown and forgotten by any witnesses. According to Beel, the only tragic note was that nobody drowned.

The same payback stunt was reported by a reader of the first volume, who said the job ended abruptly when the tent ripped loose in the middle of a bumpy road curve being taken at high speed. The tent and its marks slammed into a small tree, then rolled en masse into a mammoth briar patch. We'll just credit that one to Uncle Remus.

Campus

It seems this kid named Curry was a sneaky sort. While other students did their own term papers, Curry used to buy his already written. Or, he would hire a good journalism major to ghostwrite him an "A" paper. A couple of his peers decided some creative revenge was in order.

They plagiarized a few semi-obscure essays from some dust-covered literature books in a seldom-used portion of the university library. They had these short essays and poems typed under Curry's name and submitted them to the campus literary magazine.

Hilariously, the literary magazine adviser never saw "Curry's" essays, while the student editors had never been exposed to the obscure originals and did not recognize the scam. Thus, the plagiarized pieces went into the magazine. Within minutes of the publication's appearance on campus, the adviser was besieged by calls from distraught English department faculty members who hadn't had so much excitement since some wag suggested they elect the campus water fountain chairperson. Naturally, in the time honored academic tradition, as the effluvia hit the fan, the mess filtered downward. The puzzled mark had to go through a campus hearing and until his influential parents brought pressure on the university, the kid's future there was bleak.

This scam may be used in another way, too. The same basic plan will get a writer or reporter in trouble. Simply send plagiarized stuff in the mark's name to a professional publication. The stakes are much higher in this league, of course.

Careers

Your mark might be a college senior or might just be someone else who needs a job reference. A friend of mine used to be a college instructor, until he finally got bored with the genetic drift being admitted as undergraduates to America's campuses these days, and went back to his former occupation as a corporate personnel manager. But, his idea is a real tribute to unequal opportunity employment.

"I found out these two students had been forging my signature to all sorts of official college documents—grade change forms, class schedules, academic excuses, etc. They were advisees of mine and I felt they were violating a great academic trust and damaging that fragile student-professor relationship, not to mention the fact that the sneaky little bastards just plain pissed me off.

"A visit to the campus job placement office brought me two blank reference letter forms, and my devious sense of creative vindictiveness did the rest," he explained.

What our avenging academic did was complete a total ficticious recommendation for each offending student. He created a bogus professorial name and title, then wrote two masterfully done reference letters that absolutely sliced each student into tiny slivers. For instance, he wrote of one, "Although he may seem indolent, perhaps this is just his way of cautiously studying the situation." Or, consider this career bon mot, " _____ exhibited that good old Yankee spirit of free enterprise by offering to write term papers for his fellow students in return for money." He also wrote, "Showing knowledge outside the classroom, _____ tells me he feels the real world can be found in the barrooms, poolhalls and other social power centers within the community." My friend brought both politics and religion to his marks' reference letters, writing, "It takes guts these days to be a public advocate of atheism (student #1) Marxism (student #2), and _____ stands up boldly and loudly for what he believes in."

Our former professor says he signed the bogus reference letters and sent them to the job placement office. The clerk there duly logged them, and they were placed with the students' credentials.

"I know it worked because I had a businessman friend of mine request a copy of each student's file. My nasty reference letters were in there. My friend who got the copies for me was aghast that the 'students had been so stupid to have someone with such a poor opinion of them write a letter of recommendation.' I just smiled at that. My friend didn't know about my scam. It proved my point."

Cemetery

Once when the father of a friend of mine died, the family lawyer—supposedly a trusted "friend" of the deceased—turned out to be a real sphincter muscle, screwing up the widow's benefits and the inheritance and losing the deceased's retirement money in red tape.

Shortly after the financial disaster, my friend began to badger the telephone company and the local cemetery in the name of the lawyer, making all sorts of wild requests for a special telephone hook-up for his casket. Posing as the mark, my friend explained he had this fear of being buried alive. He kept this up for months.

Finally, the lawyer convinced the people at the telephone company and the cemetery that he was the victim of a hoax. He also sought police protection because he feared some psycho was out to kill him—the hints about caskets, death, etc. In final desperation, he called my friend and almost begged him to tell the truth—was he behind the terror tactics? My friend says he just laughed his most chilling J. R. Ewing laugh into the phone and hung up. Later that afternoon, he mailed the lawyer a "Sympathy on the death in your family" card. He did this off and on for another month.

He then went to an anti-establishment tabloid newspaper and paid them to run the lawyer's obituary as an advertisement. They were happy to do it, needing both the money and a good laugh at the discomfort of the badgered barrister. Seeing the notice, the editor of the local daily quickly called the lawyer's family "to see if all was well?" When the harried mark took his family on a sudden vacation within that week, my friend then ran an ad "in his behalf" in the local daily. The ad said the mark's law firm would be closed for several days because of a death in the family.

My friend finally quit when a friend of his, a local police investigator who was no friend of the attorney either, told him he was close to getting in trouble. My friend took the hint . . . for the time being.

Classified Ads

All good Americans are born bargain hunters, especially when the price is free. But, I had this acquaintance who was beyond amazingly cheap. I have actually seen him scarf up tips from other people's tables at restaurants. He had to be paid back, as it were.

One day I placed an ad in his local newspaper saying that my mark had free cocker spaniel puppies to give away. The following week I did it with kittens. I let him go a week, then had him giving away manure. Next, he was selling used guns that I priced about 20 percent below the normal price. I made the rounds of the local shops that allow people to post personal want ads on index cards. I started him all over again in this medium. In each message I included his telephone number and told people to call well after midnight because of shift work.

The final phase involved those classified personals in the sleazy sex publications. This worked well because this cheap mark and his wife were ultra straight, born-again religious freaks whose attitude about fun stuff was expressed in terms of "if God had wanted us to be naked, He would have had us born that way." When he began to get really kinky responses to the really kinky ads I placed in his name, the tolerance and Christian patience of his equally boring wife was stretched beyond turning her other well-padded cheek. Last I heard they were attending additional crash courses in dissolving lustful thoughts, or going cold turkey on even thinking about procreation. But, he hasn't been out in public since then to pick up someone else's tips.

Computers

According to a reader who signed his letter "Dr. Wizard," many computer systems are highly vulnerable to having self-destruct programs written into a loop. Or, he suggests you can set up and program some sort of self-perpetuating mathematical problem in astronomy, something to devour hundreds of hours of undetected-until-too-late computer time. I suggest you check your closest and most trustworthy data domain bandit about operational details. But, it would be great to do this to some deserving computer abuser.

Several readers made other suggestions for computer discomfort. One specific idea was to obtain magnetized tape of the type sold by trade name companies like Chartpac and Letraset. Place a strip of this tape over the appropriate magnetic ink computer code portions of such documents as your telephone bill, credit card bills, etc. It makes the lives of the corporate computer folks technically unpleasant and costs the establishment lots of extra money to unsnarl your mess.

Conventions

Although billed under the Convention heading, these monkey warfare ideas will work well at any conference, meeting or semi-serious gathering. They could also be used for some of those combination business/social functions that our corporate cancers love so much. The first suggestion came from the fertile mind of Col. Friedkin Maximov, propaganda officer of the Student Libertarian Army, an anarchist group of folks whose motto is "All power to the trash heap."

They pulled this gemlet off during the 1978 National Student Association and National Student Lobby conventions. Their first step was intelligence gathering about who the key officials were, where they were staying and where and when the key meetings would be held. Next, a supply of forged credentials and memoranda were gathered. Most of the memoranda were from one official to another and covered such topics as moving key meeting times and places; moving banquets ahead an hour/denying rumors of an outbreak of Legionnaires Disease; bomb threat denials; and a preliminary evacuation plan, "just in case." Dated and timed for appropriate dissemination, the memos created chaos and spread confusion and mistrust throughout the convention. Col. Maximov says it took several hours to get things under semi-control, but the bug of paranoia had been sewn.

You really don't have to be Abbie Hoffman or even Philo Freed to sabotage a convention. According to Jim Brownie, here's all you do.

"You know the current vogue is to have circus type clowns at conventions . . . decorated, and all that. There are 'Rent-A-Clown' places in most all major cities. Why not hire your own clowns?

"You get your own special pranksters, who will 'work' in addition to the real clowns. The idea is to dress yours the same way. Of course, while the establishment-convention clowns are doing gentle, good-natured stuff, your clowns are spilling people's drinks on other people, honking stuffy society matrons' boobs, pinching asses, spitting on important people, exposing themselves, handing out dirty pictures, etc."

He adds that shortly pandemonium will result, by which time you and your clowns are gone. The convention planners will garner the blame for this one, regardless of their shameless denials.

I have this friend who is a minor league Ted Turner, in that while Turner enjoys expensive wine, women, song and athletic competition, my pal digs booze, broads, boogie and sports. He told me how he once got chewed out by the executive director of his professional association, a very stuffy sort—I know the man, too—for coming drunk to a convention dinner and burping a few times. He also nuzzled his wife openly. I mean, what the hell, he didn't pinch her banquet buns or anything. Anyway, he caught

hell from this pious old poop. A seed of revenge hatched that very evening. My friend took six months to set up his scam. He waited until the association's Fall meeting.

"I hired a very attractive and uninhibited couple, a call girl and a sex film performer, to attend the association dinner. I purchased guest tickets for them in the name of the executive director. She wore a gown right off the rack at Frederick's of Hollywood. She looked great. So did the stud she came with. They attracted a lot of attention just in looks.

"As the executive director started his usual, boring 30 minute pre-dinner monotone, my ringers started to nuzzle each other. Within moments, attention left the podium and was zeroed in on my hired couple. They were panting away, kissing with their tongues tied around each others. Then, the guy's hand pops into the loose gown and out comes a breast to be played with. You can guess where his other hand goes next. She's groaning and tugging at his pants, moaning about how much she wants to 'voluntarily perform an unnatural sex act' (that sort of wording keeps my editor happy) on him.

"I'm not joking, before anyone could make a move, his pants are off and he hoists her right up on the table and they start going at it. No lie, it was great, they were really going at it. My wife and I started to applaud. So did a few other young couples. Our association director almost had a stroke. His wife (they deserve each other) fainted. Anyway he killed the lights in the hall, which, of course, just added to the confusion.

"I was high on humor and started to throw food. So did other folks. Without going into more detail, let me assure you the rest of the convention died at that point. It was the funniest thing I have ever seen and the greatest thing I have ever done in the name of personal freedom. The executive director has never lived that one down . . . even today, six years later."

Corporations

Although this scam will work best with large corporations, you could adapt it to smaller companies or organizations as well. Obviously, by this far into our dirty tricks alphabet, you must know that you should have just cause for your revenge!

After your basic intelligence gathering and planning stage, you need to acquire an original and official letterhead and envelope from the mark. One way to obtain that letterhead/envelope is to innocently write the company for information. Or, visit the offices and swipe some during a lunch hour or just at quitting time. A good Xerox-type machine and some skills explained in Volume I will give you your own supply of "official" letterhead. Or, your friendly printer could do the same thing.

Next, using that new letterhead, write a sharply worded business letter from Company A to Company B, demanding payment for merchandise, equipment, etc. Then, using Company B's "official" letterhead, write Company A a nasty letter complaining of faulty merchandise, equipment, etc., and threatening personal injury damages from same.

In your research and intelligence phase you need to obtain the names and, if possible, the signatures of some middle managers who will "sign" your letters. Now, you mail them and await the communication fun.

Credit Cards

Recently, a straight friend told me that Montgomery Ward was now requiring all charge card customers to personally present cards and signatures on the spot because so much fraud from phoned in orders with phoney numbers, or from folks who had "forgotten their cards." Ahahahah, more readers of **Get Even** strike again and again. Delightful.

But, here's an update angle to this problem. If you still have the number of your mark's card, you can still order all sorts of expensive things on those toll free mail order telephone numbers. I asked an acquaintance who works for one of the large mail order houses about this.

"Our volume of incoming calls precludes any sort of even cursory check until after the materials are on their way. We advertise fast service and to be competitive we just have to take the chance. We base that on the fact that 95 percent of our customers are the real thing."

The secret for you is to join the 5 percent of rotters who are having all the fun, getting all the goodies, or who are ordering all the wrong goodies for their marks.

My friend noted reluctantly, "You've seen our spots on TV . . . 'Simply pick up your phone and dial now . . . operators on duty . . . call toll free . . . ' that's it."

Take his word for it. If you use a good mail drop, as I explained in the first book, this is a great way to get free records, books, pots, pans, food, and also, X-rated videocassettes. Or, you can order not only with your mark's credit card number, but in his or her name and address.

Dead Bodies

Sorry, I didn't know what else to call this one, as it really doesn't involve human cadavers. But, let Abe Mirthal explain—it was his idea in the first place.

"When I went to Virginia Beach and other Atlantic coastal resorts, I used to see an oceanic novelty in the various souvenir shops. It was something known as a sea-monkey or devilfish. The novelty was the dried-up skin of this creature. It looked strikingly like a tiny, shriveled-up human body."

Abe suggests that you may know someone who would be horrified to see or receive one of these creatures dressed in soiled doll clothing or some other format/scenario that might be appropriate. As always, think of some way to make your punishment fit the mark's crime against you. Perhaps you can use Abe's creatures to get even some way.

The only time he personally knew of this being used was to terrorize a child molester who had hired an oily attorney to get him out of the charges. Both the molester and his accomplice, the legal hitman, got several exposures to these horrid visions. Word is the molester soon moved to another city and the attorney limited himself to corporate practice—which hardly seems like contrition to me!

Disguise

Watching television can be beneficial to your creative revenge. On "The Tonight Show," super-American Jimmy Stewart told Johnny Carson about a chemical called bichloride of mercury, which will give the user a sore throat, altering the sound of the voice. Stewart used it to make his voice hoarse in the film "Mr. Smith Goes to Washington." I bet you could figure out all sorts of interesting uses for that stuff, either for yourself or for your mark. For example, think of the fun if your mark was a singer or a politician or businessman giving an important speech . . . and prior to the event you slipped some bichloride of mercury to that person.

Drugs

Two readers of my initial literary effort wrote to tell me that Yohimbine really is a medical aphrodisiac. One, a pharmacist, says it really will work. It is used by veteriniarians and if handled carefully would be both safe and effective with humans. The key word he stressed was safety. I wonder if that is before or after the inclusion of the drug? The other reader claimed to be a "field tester." He didn't say of what. In any case, his terse message was, "Yohimbine is the real thing. It can really buzz up a chick."

Contributor Ellen James writes that her idea is more of a practical joke than a dirty trick. But, it's nothing to snort at because it's sure to tweak the noses of some marks. In any case, the scene is one of those posh cocaine settings where everyone is "oh so ready to do a few lines." You gently smuggle a bit of milk sugar in your place in line, as it were. When it's your turn to pull 'er in . . . you suddenly choke, puff, then sneeze like fury . . . blowing the milk sugar all over the atmosphere. The heads think you've just wasted umpteen dozen dollars worth of coke. And, well, as she said, it's more of a joke. The ending's up to you.

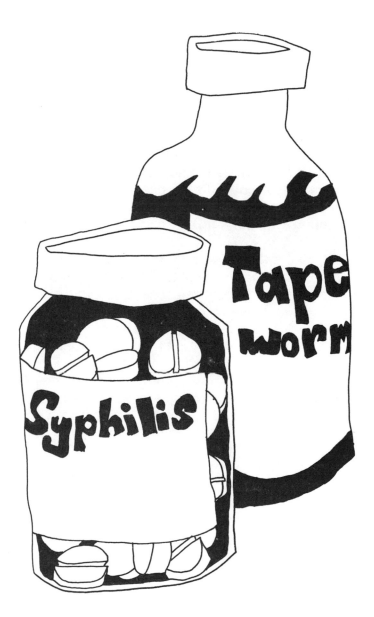

Fifteen U.S. Air Force officers and enlisted men assigned to operate a nuclear missile silo in Arizona were suspended from duty after two joints of potent marijuana were discovered by security guards on the control room floor. Think of the possibilities for sabotage. Think of the possibilities for planting evidence to incriminate your mark.

Another reader passed along the nature lore that Hawaiian Baby Woodrose seeds, *Argyreia nervosa,* are a potent hallucinogen. He also claims that common Morning Glories can be distilled into a homemade LSD-like concoction. Have a good trip, because some other folks are on a bad journey now.

Malcolm Miller was simply a middle class pissant, until he turned in some friends who were making private and moderate use of *cannibis sativa* among themselves. After paying a moderate fine and getting suspended sentences from some drunken hypocrite of a Nixonian judge, our heroes decided to get back at their pot pooper.

They obtained some medicine bottles of the type in which prescriptions are dispensed. One of them lifted a pad of prescription labels from a small pharmacy. They typed labels in the name of the mark, then included the instructions, "Take one every four hours for penis infection." They also typed labels for him, "infecting" him with pinworms, VD, trenchmouth, alcoholism, opiate reaction, herpes, etc. The bottles began to appear around his area at work, in his car, in his wife's car, etc.

Electrical

If this bit hadn't come from former CIA man Miles Kendig I would put it down as a shocking parlor trick that will short out your mark's lights.

Here's how it works. Select a **wall switch operated** electrical appliance that will conduct the trick for your mark, such as a table lamp, TV set, stereo, table top oven, etc. Make certain the power switch is in the OFF mode. Then, pull out the appliance's plug from the wall receptacle. Take a steel paperclip and place each end of the clip over the two prongs on the appliance's male plug. Slide the steel paperclip down to the base of the plug. Plug the appliance back in. Do NOT turn on the power mode switch; leave that for your mark. When he or she hits the power switch . . . KABLOOOEY . . . a violently major short circuit takes place, and all sorts of things blow out. Miles says if you're lucky you might get a whole house outage from this trick.

Elevators

After the first book came out I did a lot of radio and TV interviews because many media people thought my concept of getting even was fairly amusing. Several of the interviewers got into the spirit of my creative revenge and suggested their own ideas for this second volume. Many of those are in this book. But, only a few of the media people would allow me to use names. So, here goes one of them.

David Hall of WQXI in Atlanta once had reason to be furious with the administrators of his college during undergraduate days. The beef had to do with visiting hours, curfews and a high-rise dormitory building. A nonengineer, Hall spent one hour rewiring the floor indicator buttons behind the electric panel behind the floor indicator buttons of the dorm's elevator.

Hall says, "I rewired buttons and stops so the floors and the indicators didn't match. For example, someone would punch the button for 5 and end up on 10. Or, they'd hit 8 and end up on 2, things like that. I did it on Saturday night when everyone was likely to come late and drunk. It was hilarious."

Even more hilarious was Hall's report that it took the university's electricians an entire day to get the machine coordinated again.

Employer

Want to get your tax money's worth out of an employer who's done you dirty? An earnest, "decent citizen doing his or her duty" telephone call to OSHA, the state health authorities, or the local fire inspector will get results in the form of a safety inspection. Even if the mark's place is clean, which is probably only a 50/50 shot from what I've seen while moving about the country, the bureaucratic harassment will not be appreciated in the least. The paperwork for even the innocent is staggering and expensive. If you strike it lucky, there will be an investigation and hearing.

Fish

I never knew how emotional people were about aquariums and tropical fish life until I heard a person at a party tearfully tell how the heater in his tank malfunctioned and turned that watery world into a large fish fry. Amazing.

If for some reason you want to get back at one of these fish fanatics, you could always slip a few Alka Seltzer in the tank. Or, if you were of a more terminal mind, try adding some small water snakes to that closed environment. You could also hook up a current activator or submersible heater to your mark's room light switch. That way, when he or she comes in and hits the light switch, they act as the executioner.

Food

Labels come off food cans very easily, according to Margaret Dayton, kindly contributor to this volume. If you can get to the mark's food supply, switch and reglue some of the labels, e.g., Campbell's Beef Chunks and Alpo could switch labels. Margaret cautions though that your mark may be such a slob as to not notice the difference. But, I bet the mark's dog will.

If you can't get into the mark's home, try to slip the switched dog food labeled as Beef Chunks into his or her shopping cart after he or she has checked out of the local market.

Margaret adds this same stunt can be used to gain revenge against a supermarket which has done something to deserve retribution.

An ice cream cone will go well on any day. If your mark likes ice cream, here's an idea. Collect a live cockroach or two, and put them into the cone before you have the ice cream packed in. Imagine his or her surprise when half a roach is spotted sticking out of a fresh bite out of the ice cream.

One of my good friends who also works for my publisher suggested this idea, and its pretty darned

funny, to me. Basically, what you're doing is getting back at a vegetarian who has done you dirty. Because these people are so dedicated to their anti-meatism, this trick usually works well.

My friend advises, "You just slip some bits of pork into their veggie food. It works well in salad, stews and soups. But, save some evidence so you can prove it. It's wonderful, especially if they've just hogged out on a whole load of your doctored food and are really devout vegetarians."

He reported in one instance where he saw this done, the mark lost his entire dinner—on the spot.

Foreign Officials

According to an AP story appearing late in 1980, American news people assigned to the Soviet Union found a lovely way to destroy the bureaucratic hassle created by officious Kremlin minions. When some Soviet official becomes a pain in the tass, the news hawks attack.

"We have colleagues who are in exotic places like Hong Kong, Tokyo, or Paris send colorful, exciting postal cards to those nasty officials," one of the newsmen told me.

"The cards say things like 'Your exposé manuscript arrived safely,' or 'money deposited in your Swiss account,' or something suspiciously cryptic like, 'The sun is out and the water is fine.' Knowing how terminally paranoid Soviet officials are, the cards get wonderful results despite being so obvious. Soviet officialdom has no sense of humor."

A number of obvious variations come to mind involving domestic politicians, military or law enforcement officials. Can you imagine what you could do to some self-esteemed Narc, BATF or IRS goon with a card like that? How's a Cuban postmark sound? There are re-mailing services that would help you in this scam.

Early in 1981, jubilant journalists revealed other caustic coups which duped the Soviet nasties. Some journalists took their revenge to delightful extremes.

One man sent a package of banned books to an official, but addressed the parcel to a different department. When the package was opened it set off an investigation that involved the official's friends and family.

Another journalist sent a card to a KGB agent who had been harassing him.

It read: "Please deposit the 100 rubles gambling debt you owe me in my Moscow bank account."

Then he asked a friend to deposit 100 rubles into his bank account, with the policeman's name on the deposit slip.

The policeman was eventually cleared . . . for the time being, anyway.

As my journalistic friend remind, "In every Communist country, allegations of corruption, however improbable, are investigated with relentless energy."

Gasoline

In his excellent book *They Were Expendable*, W. L. White writes about the first few months of WWII as it affected the men of a motor torpedo boat squadron. One segment of the book described a Japanese agent who sabotaged the American PT boats by pouring dissolved candle wax into their gasoline drums. Running this mixture through the engines created all sorts of nasty hell with filters, critical tolerances, etc. You don't have to be of the Japanese persuasion or even at war to adapt this gimmick to your mark's gasoline supply or even to his automobile, boat, tractor, snowmobile, or whatever. It would work in a gasoline-powered generator, too, and in just about any engine powered by a petroleum fuel. That should brighten the light of your creative candle and allow you to wax eloquently upon this new use of this old dirty trick. Banzai!

Graffiti

If you must graffit, do it with some thought. If, for example, you scrawl foul words and gross sayings on some bridge overpass, a public building, or a highway department storage dome, the cleaning crews are going to be hustled right out to scrub off your artwork. But, if you use subtle phrasing and upper class language, you can still get across the point of your message, and it is likely to stay around longer. Bland is not a priority item in cleaning up Puritan America; Anglo-Saxon obscenity is.

For example, spying fresh cement, don't scrawl DICK NIXON FELLATES DEAD ANIMALS, or NIXON REALLY IS A DICK. That's gross. Instead, write DICK NIXON REALLY IS A CROOK. Or, NIXON IN '84; WHY NOT A LOSER. I know it's not as funny, but it will have a longer traffic life. Guaranteed! After years of study, I know the bureaucratic mind, as well as graffiti.

Gun Control

Once, in another life, I was co-hosting a cutesy-tootsie cocktail party when an archtypical Loonie Liberal couple started passing around a "Ban the Guns" petition. Being a sensitive, polite sort even then, I quietly informed them that such political activity in my home offended me and would they please desist. Instead, I got more anti-gun pitch tinged with a hysteria about "our" being an elite group of opinion formers, whatever that is, and how vital it is that guns be banned. I was told this issue was more important than my own feelings.

My hand shot out, grabbed the petition, tore it in half then pitched both halves into the fireplace. I smiled and said, "Let the party continue, friends." From that point on, I have refused to party with activist Liberals or Conservatives. Neither are worth a bag of manure. I now party only with fellow drunks and heads.

But, my act of momentary violence was not really getting even. The petition destroying response was not the end of that party incident. After a cooling off period, because like many activists, my anti-gun mark and his lady had limited attention spans, I started a little revenge campaign.

I bought some plastic handguns at a large discount store and began to place one in their mailbox, or tape it to their apartment door at night every ten days or so. Once, I put one in on their car seat, then reported to police about "a car with a handgun on the seat in plain view." That created some real fun.

Using a postal money order I got my mark a year's membership in the National Rifle Association —faking the membership application a bit, of course. I pledged a huge amount in his name to all the "Right to Bear Arms" groups. He thus became the recipient of a large volume of mail particularly noxious to him.

He didn't change his mind, of course, but I heard through a third party that my mark was "furious" about someone's harassing him. But, he guessed "it was the price to pay for being controversial." To help his anxiety, I started doing the things on a more random basis—one month on, two off, one on, three off, two on, things like that.

The pro-gun baboons are just as bad, usually being illiterate as well. If you don't believe me, just read some of the letters in their various publications. I worry about some of them being allowed to drive cars, hold jobs, have children, and vote, much less owning firearms. But, I digress. . . .

A reader who farms wrote to tell me about having to chase slob hunters away from his house each and every deer season. A few give him a really bad time, which is why he reluctantly posted his 100 acres of prime woodland and lush cornfields. After one "sportsman" made a strong verbal threat backed with his rifle, my correspondent started his campaign. He got the hunter's vehicle license number and had a friend with the local police run down a name and address to go with it. It checked out.

"In addition to the usual goodies I picked up from your first book and used, I added a few of my own," this man wrote me. "I legally bought some submachine gun parts I saw advertised in a gun publication. At night I entered the man's backyard and buried the parts, wrapped in heavy plastic, in his garden.

"I knew this guy bragged how he could get guns for people without paperwork and at wholesale. So, I had a friend of mine who knows the gun business meet with the mark at a gun show and buy some handguns from him. There was no entrapment or strawman stuff—the mark sold illegally and outright for cash.

"I then called the regional BATF office and complained about what I had seen at the gunshow. You know the BATF! They gestapoized the mark. After the mark had gone through this and nearly had his entire collection confiscated by those federal nasties, I had another person tip our local police about the mark trafficking in machine guns. The tip included some information about the garden. You can imagine how that day dawned when the feds and the locals closed in on the mark."

What this man did was extreme and perhaps he overdid it. I have no love for the fascist swine at BATF. But, I also have no love for a slob who points a gun at someone else and/or threatens to use it. You takes your chances, as someone once pointed out.

Hawkers

Don't read this section unless you are (1) gross, (2) have a strong stomach, (3) have a terminally bizarre sense of humor, or (4) all of the above. Thanks to Chris Scott, we now have a creative use for hawkers. See, I warned you! It's not too late to turn back a few sentences. Very well.

Hawkers are especially yukky specimens of phlegm which one hawks up from the nether regions of the throat and the waste canals of the nasal passages. According to Scott, a hawker is an especially gooey mass of phlegm containing enough multi-colored solids to make it an effective missile.

A dirty trickster can use hawkers in a plebian sense, or he may operate with some creative class. For example, it is possible, Scott tells me, to quietly deposit a few hawkers in glassware at cafeterias and restaurants. When an innocent customer selects the anointed vessel he will be horrified, sickened and will probably make this fact loudly known to your mark—the management of the restaurant.

In direct attack, which is not especially subtle and could invite physical retribution, the hawker is propelled directly upon the mark. Scott says that only choice hawkers should be used for this purpose and that a careful intelligence analysis should be made of the mark, the target area and setting. According to a former Major League baseball pitcher, one of his teammates was exceptionally adept at this trick, and once made another teammate physically sick by sloppily depositing an especially horrible mixutre of hawker and chewing tobacco on the man's arm. The horrified teammate who received this offering ran for the bathroom and spent the next few minutes embracing the commode while spilling his lunch into the bowl.

Horses

As every country boy and a few of the older generation of ex-college students know, you can lead a horse up a staircase. But, it's pure hell to try to get that horse to come back down again. Maybe this is also true of cattle, swine, sheep, goats, etc. I don't know if it is. Surely someone can put this random bit of equestrian trivia to good use on some mark somewhere.

Hotels, Motels, and High Rises

This one came in from Gabe Torquato because he was angry at a hotel that quartered him in a room directly above the grand ballroom where a convention of vets was trying to sound like the Battle of the Bulgies. His revenge was so simplistic and slapstick that I was not going to use it. But, the sillier it got, the more impressive the idea became. Read on.

His original idea was to go to random room areas of the hotel and drop large plastic bags of water out of windows on convention delegates. Simple stuff—most high school kids are veterans of that one. But, I began to think about deeper implications. Suppose you add rubber toy rats or snakes to the bag of liquid? Suppose you use urine? Suppose you mixed feces in with the water? Suppose you mixed in canned vegetable soup, so it would look like vomit? Or, you could jettison bags of paint. Or, bags of exceptionally overripe roadkill.

While your primary mark is the hotel management, you are, of course, inflicting severe emotional distress upon those poor random targets down below. As the pain and shock of getting hit with God-knows-what builds, so will the paranoia of "Why Me? Why was I Chosen for This Attack?"

from the Master of Revenge

One of Aunt Bertie's nephews told me about
this one. He was staying at a motel in Memphis
(sounds like a rock song title) on the same floor as a
convention of very uptight Bible Bangers who spent
half his sleepless night trying to save him, and pray-
ing for his lost soul. Actually, all he had lost by then
was a night's sleep and his patience. The management merely "tut tutted" a feeble apology, but
refused to enforce quiet on the Lord's people.

The next morning, before checking out, Aunt
Bertie's nephew used a razorblade to cut a small
hiding hole into the pages of the Gideon Bible in his
room. Closed, it looked like any other bible. Open it
up and you'll find the two packets of condoms that
dear nephew stashed there, along with a note "from"
the Motel Management, written on a memo pad he'd
filched at the desk during his nighttime complaint
session. The note told the religious folks to use the
rubbers to "get it up so they could get it on with a
really religious experience." He signed it, St. Peter,
lay minister, order of St. Mattress."

A traveling man, the dear nephew has done the
same basic trick to other motels which displease
him, sometimes substituting dope, booze, porno, a
guide to local hookers or gay bars for the condoms.

"Once I went to a blue-nosed, fundamentalist
'temple' and taped porno pictures in their hymnals,
right there in the church itself. I loved it and I bet
some of the good parishoners did too on the next
Sunday," he recalled.

Ahh yes, do unto others after they have done
unto you. But, doeth yours twice as hard and nasty!

House Plants

I have this friend named Pangle, whose bossy roommate used to bitch all the time because Pangle would forget to water roomie's plants while roomie was out playing Jacques Cousteau on some friend's sailboat. Pangle figured the old salt needed some rubbing in, so she began to carry out the order of her admirable roommate. She used salt water, a look of total innocence, then feigned sorrow when the plants failed to survive the saline watering voyage.

Along the same line, getting to the root of a personality conflict, one obviously henpecked reader noted that his domineering mother used to force him to keep her house plants cleaned, watered and cared for. He hated the plants, which is probably unfair, because I suspect it was his mother he really didn't like. Anyway, he started to mix food coloring in with the water he used on the plants.

"Within a week my mother had plants with colored 'veins' running through the stems and leaves. I convinced her they were very sick plants. She dismissed my care as incompetent and took over herself. That's all I needed."

He added a postscript that the plants died. His mother bought all new specimens and would not allow junior near them. I wondered as I read his letter again if he ever thought of putting food coloring in his mother's drinks.

Households

Kenny Braun had a nice little puppy that he kept in a roomy, chicken wire enclosure of some 200 square feet with a solid, comfortable doghouse in the center. He fed and watered his pup daily, plus his kids played with it a lot. It had a great life in its little environment.

Then, there was the next door neighbor, Lorrie Miller, who had a big, bully, nasty Doberman that had to live up to its reputation. It used to trespass into Braun's place and terrorize both the kids and the puppy. After many wasted attempts to dissuade Miller from this folly, Braun took other action.

"I filled a balloon with urine, then went next door and hurled it through the screen door so it would splatter all over the new carpet inside on the living room. The Doberman came loping into the room, sniffed my splashy results, and started 'marking' all over the carpet area, trying to reestablish his territory."

If you need a lesson on dog territoriality, they mark the borders of their property by spraying copious amounts of urine. Ever see a dog hit a tree or a bush? They are usually marking territory. Needless to say, the Miller dog spent days trying to overcome

Braun's repeated urine-filled balloon attacks. Soon, the expensive new carpet fell victim to this odorous and acidic assault. The Doberman got full credit, and was soon penned up. Such is a dog's life.

Lawns

In the first book I suggested writing nasty words on lawns with weed killer. A reader suggested one can substitute weed killer for insecticide in your mark's garden supply chemicals. That way, when he sprays for cutworms or grubs he will defoliate everything. I can think of several deserving people who would die if their roses fell victim to this old product switcheroo when they thought they were spraying for Japanese beetles.

This one will work for as long as your mark is gullible or patriotic Dump an exceedingly large, cumbersome, ugly, and odd-shaped piece of concrete on your mark's property or lawn. You have affixed to it a very authentic looking metal label which reads, "'U.S. Government Time Capsule—Do Not Remove Under Penalty of Federal Law. U.S. Department of the Interior."

Naturally, the mark's telephone calls will go out to Washington and the bureaucrats at Interior will bustle like an ant farm, shuffling papers and passing the buck slips along. Be sure you notify local news media. Stuff like this is big news to small newspapers and radio stations. I suspect the mark will take care of notifying local police—who will probably not do anything because of jurisdictional problems, i.e., "a federal case." If you're lucky, the FBI, your mark's congressman, and some big city media will be involved before it's all over.

Lawyers

The **Get Even** series legal adviser, Orlon Spectre, has a fun use for a quitclaim deed. Like its name suggests, this is a document that allows you, or your mark, to relinquish all actual and potential interest in some described piece of property. You use it by getting some lawyer to have his secretary write something like, "I hereby grant to _____ all my interests, present and future, in the following described personal property. . . ."

In the law according to Hayduke, you can send your mark quitclaim deeds notarized in all sorts of pompous formality (see **Get Even**) with all sorts of donations to him. It will confuse, bewilder and frighten the usual mark. Or, you can have your mark give away any and all of his property to some charity, real or bogus. Just send the charity his quitclaim deed. Or, send the charity the document and send him a copy. In either case you will create far more confusion and elevated blood pressure than the entire document is worth.

Spectre also suggests you rope in the local news media by getting publicity out of using a quitclaim deed to provide some bogus or unpopular charity with ownership of some valuable piece of property sure to stir up the public unrest, e.g. deed-ing the town square of Skokie, Ill. to the American Nazi party. He also suggests that if you want to make your own heirs unhappy by delaying the division of your Will, include some outrageous quitclaim deeds in that document.

Letterhead

Howard Paper Mills, Inc. found commercial graffiti, consumer alienation and their own letterhead designs a viable, but novelty, marketing combination. In 1980, they promoted the clever gimmick of letterheads for angry people. Basically, the deal was to show off Howard's line of printing papers to people who use a lot of paper stock, e.g. printers, advertising people, etc. Yet, the appeal was to the upset soul like you who'd read **Get Even 2.**

They put out expensive sample kits showing actual "stock" letterhead and matching envelopes for various categories of angry public letter writers. For example, their first packet showed a naked, irate taxpayer in a barrel shaking his fist at the IRS. This letterhead is printed on what faintly appears to be an IRS form 1040. A second design was a heart with a hole in it . . . for a jilted lover. Another clever design is a "folded, spindled, and mutilated, shafted, electronically, Inc." reproduction of our ubiquitous friend, the computer card, in a letterhead motif.

They have a really hilarious one for people whose autos have been crunched in parking lot combat. It's headed "The Door-Dented and Apoplectic Parking Lot Patrons, Anonymous." A final specimen in hot red ink and a headline reading "FURIOUS" in big, shaky letters.

The first set was so successful they issued a second edition of spleen-venting stationery. One is a "Don't Tread on Me" warning to government bureaucrats; there is a David and Goliath theme; another letterhead for TV program critics; a really great one to send to the makers of shoddy and sleazy products; plus one for sexist pigs. Later, this fun-thinking Dayton, Ohio, paper company opened its graffitorial efforts to the public in an "Angry American" contest. No, I did not enter ... theirs was for amateurs.

Libraries

Juan McMann didn't even own a library card. He'd never even been in the library. Yet, he received an overdue book/fine letter from the very same library he'd never been in. His telephoned explanations were abused and he was insulted. He was threatened again. He finally had to spend $50 to hire an attorney to set the record straight. He cursed the damn library.

Juan spent another $50 having some book titleplates printed. Titleplates are snobbish gum-backed labels that announce a book's title, author and donor. Juan had some very pornographic, bogus title plates printed, and pasted them in old classics at his favorite library. I will leave to your imagination just how clinically disgusting his choices were. He's a very grossly creative man, and his specific ideas don't belong in a book of this nature.

Do yours?

Locks

Several readers complained that when they tried to pump Epoxy into locks using a pressure gun or a syringe, the stuff hardened unless they used it quickly. One of my favorite friends and chemists came up with the no-pun solution. Gino Sanford suggests mixing the Epoxy with some form of alcohol before putting the stuff into the syringe. He says many alcohols will work to retard the curing process until you're ready to use it. The exposure to air will start the evaporation of the alcohol and the curing of the Epoxy.

Luggage, Briefcases, and the Like

I can't think of an actual scenario, but you never know when it would be fun to ground your mark's luggage, parcels or briefcase to a floor somewhere. If you find yourself in this delightful dilemma, I suggest a nail gun, such as the Hilti or a Ramset. You can literally shoot and fasten someone's luggage securely to a cement slab floor. Or, use one of the many Epoxy products, if you can guarantee an overnight setting time. They'll never get it up—the product, that is.

Lust

Remember that lustful jerk from the first book? Angie Spencer suggests another way of dealing with him. Being a gentleman I didn't ask her motivation or rationale for such a mean trick. But, it's a goodie.

You need to enlist the help of a great looking lady with a sense of humor and an equally together guy who could pass for female with some work. You dress them both to look as sexy as can be without getting arrested, paying attention to the physical specifics your mark will like.

You have a party, the mark has a party or someone has a party to which they invite you and the mark. No one ever cares if two single ladies just happen to show up at a party.

Since your mark is a lecher to begin with, it will be no problem for the real girl to come on to him, being sure to see he is fed as much alcohol or drugs or both as possible. When the time seems right, the real girl introduces her girl friend—your fake girl— to the mark. The two "girls" offer to "go upstairs for a good time threesome." The Dirty Old Man will jump at the chance, hopefully.

Once upstairs, the entire plan will have to proceed on an ad-lib basis with your two assistants playing the thing by ear, so to speak. But, the ideal is to get the mark as naked as possible, with the real girl keeping him as interested as possible. Meanwhile, the fake girl has moved behind the mark and removed "her" skirt. She then pulls down her female panties enough to expose "her" male sexual apparatus. You jump into the room at this point, from the hall or the closet, however you three have set up the mark, and snap a picture. You now have your mark dead hard and cold—on film.

If you are very sophisticated you can use infrared film and flash lighting that won't give any visual signal that pictures are being taken. Or, if the room is well lighted enough, go for available light photography with a good 35mm and fast film.

Remember how I suggested in the first **Get Even** about the gambit of planting sexy underwear? A reader suggests substituting those cutesy white laced-flower stockings worn by junior high aged girls. He suggests planting them early in the school term so the mark's wife has timely cause for concern about her old man hustling some pubescent cutie. It's stuff like this that causes the funniest letters to "Dear Abby."

Particularly if you're a woman, you'll smile as I did at this next perverse piece on current anti-rape technology.

An Arizona inventor by the name of Charles Barlow has come up with a nifty little anti-rape device which now carries a U.S. Patent Office registration number. In effect, he has developed a *vagina harpoona,* a mechanized version of that old male nightmare *vagina dentata.*

Mr. Barlow's vaginal harpoon is a tiny base housing a tinier yet compressible coil spring covered with a soft plastic cloth. A thin reed of surgical steel with a pointed, harpoon-like tip is embedded in the center of the coil.

The device is inserted into the vagina with aid of a tube and a lubricant, much the same as a tampon. When the vagina is visited by an unwanted male, the coil is compressed and the harpoon is activated, solidly impaling the intruder's member on his first thrust. The inventor claims that when the horribly pained male quickly withdraws, he pulls the contraption out with him due to the barbed tip of the harpoon.

The inventor also claims that professional medical assistance will be required to remove the device safely, which will enable a doctor to identify a rapist to the appropriate authorities. I don't know if this device has gone beyond the prototype stage or if it has been used in actual field service. A call to Mr. Barlow got me a "no comment." I was afraid to ask to speak to Mrs. Barlow, heeding that old saw about watching my tongue. Perhaps, this is the ultimate answer to the problem of women always getting shafted.

Mafia

The Mob is like the weather in that everyone talks about it, but. . . . Everyone knows someone in La Cosa Nostra, right? Every Italian family semi-brags of an uncle, cousin, or someone not too close, who's connected, right? At best, the contact is a numbers runner. Usually, it's some holster-sniffing braggart who drinks coffee in the same shop the local organization's soldiers do. But, as Marshall McLuhan taught, reality doesn't matter, it's what people think.

Marcia Springchurch is a good friend of mine who once had a problem with a male subordinate. He refused to take orders from a woman. He got nasty and started the usual dirty lies about how a gorgeous young woman gets into an executive position so quickly. Marcia is a very clever lady in the vengeance area.

She made a prearranged telephone call to another friend, making her end of the conversation seem as if she were talking to some Mob enforcer. She knew her problem-boy was listening to her as his desk was less than a dozen feet away. She did a poor sotto voce bit of trying to hide what she wanted, but made it clear she wanted some "contract work done." She glanced at her mark, acted

shocked that he was listening, mumbled something about "can't talk now," and hung up. She looked flushed and left the room A seed of paranoia was planted in his pea-sized brain.

Starting that weekend, two door-filling hulks called on the troublemaker in his apartment, at his favorite disco bar and, once, after work in the company parking lot. They made it very clear that his lies about his female boss had displeased someone very powerful and important. They told him he was an unimportant worm that nobody would miss. They gave him two weeks to get a new job and get out of town, while he could still do so without the aid of an ambulance.

"It's gonna be tough for you to do the kinda work you do, pal, if we hafta come back and rip your arms out at the shoulder. And we will, we will," they told the quaking mark.

He beat their deadline by a week.

You should know that Marcia's two heavies were not really Mob muscle. They were a couple of her out of town friends who gleefully agreed to play the role. They made no illegal threats in front of witnesses, nor did they carry weapons. They simply looked, dressed and played the role of what people think a Mob musclepower soldier is supposed to look and act like.

As a postscript, Marcia says that a real Mob type she really did know found out about her actors and thought it was a hilarious scheme. He also told her that he would have made a couple of his boys—the real thing—available if necessary.

Mannequins

Store mannequins can be recruited into your dirty tricks army to frighten deserving marks. Attend a going-out-of-business sale and buy the store mannequins. You can dress them in Salvation Army, Goodwill, or thrift shop clothing. Or, leave them naked if your mission would benefit from that style of exposure. You can use these silent sentinels for all sorts of vengeful mischief.

In one instance, a reader of the first volume reported to me that he terrorized a lawyer who had screwed him out of money in a will probate case. The reader placed naked mannequins on the mark's lawn, in his car and in the hallway outside his office. He mutilated the genital areas and wrote voodoo symbols and occult signs on the bodies of the store dummies using runny red paint for bloody lookalike. He made-up the faces to look like that of the lawyer and his family. The harried lawyer finally went to the police, totally convinced a dangerous lunatic was after him.

Mass Transit

I don't know how useful this is, but someone named Terry the Tramp, who says he used to ride with Hell's Angels, related that you can make a hellish sound, and shake up the citizens, not to mention the driver, by rolling a large, metal trash can under the wheels of a city bus.

"It makes a sound like a real bad accident, man," he said. "It sounds like one of the little compact cars got crunched by the bus, run over, then dragged along."

It works best at dusk or during the first half light of early morning rush hour. I bet if you added a few "bloody" mannequins to the mess you could increase the scene's tensions.

Media

Because I travel a lot, I read many newspapers from all over the country. Most of them are pretty sad examples of journalism, dedicated more to making money as part of their community's commercial establishment than to raising needed hell. Too many American newspapers are upper middle-aged Republicans whose publishers junket with the very thieves they should be exposing. Usually, these rightwing propaganda sheets hire like-minded people to write for them. Here's where you can have some fun.

Read the local editorials and columns. Most are written by congenital defects whose idea of progress is the team of Ronald Reagan, Gerald Ford and Dwight Eisenhower, two of whom are dead. Find out the issues which really irritate the mark (an editor, publisher or columnist), then place that person's name on as many mailing lists as possible to receive junk mail propaganda favorable to that hated cause.

For example, there is an unminded old biddy writing for one smalltown paper I sometimes read. One day I saw her column she was getting hysterical about Madalyn Murray O'Hair and Atheism. It was obvious the dumbo didn't even understand Atheism, much less know how to spell Mrs. O'Hair's name. An acquaintance of mine spent an amused hour filling out postal card after postal card, addressing them to every atheist rights organization he could find, asking for information in the biddy's name. Later, he had a lady friend call many of the same groups and offer the mark's time, money and volunteer support. He suggested they all contact her at the newspaper office during working hours. The friend suggested editorial support.

Meanwhile, over on the radio side, credit goes to Steve Allen (yup, the very same one of stardom fame) for this one. Steve says to select some old dog-eared commercial that's been broadcast scores of times. This one has to be a live commercial and not one on an automatic tape cartridge. Retype the copy carefully on station copysheets, except that the last few lines are complete nonsense, or contain a strangely worded message that's not what the sponsor or the announcer intended. Or, it could be rude . . . or worse.

Make your new copy look dog-eared and messy, put the traffic stamps and initials on it to make it look authentic, then slip it into the commercial book for the DJ whose shift you want to sabotage. It works well because most radio people simply read the words and seldom pay attention to what they're reading—especially on an old piece of copy.

Your mark here is either the DJ, the sponsor, or both. In any case, Steve Allen says this trick is more fun than a barrelful of complaints from angry sponsors.

114

Military

As one of those men stereotyped as "A Vietnam Era Veteran" with an honorable discharge from the U.S. Army, I am obviously a patriot. It is with extreme reluctance that I even mention the details of how some pinko sickie is harassing the U.S. military establishment and its quota-busting headhunters. However. . . .

Former PFC (retd) Delmonte Anderson notes that he believed the recruiters when they soothed him with their snakeoil salesman's rhetoric and signed him on a khaki-colored line.

"A big mistake," Anderson confirms. "They lied about what training I'd get, where I'd be stationed and what I would do. In short, I ended up as a rifleman in a line company in Korea in 1977. I had been told I would become an electronic technician and be stationed in the States."

Judging from the fact that he was only a PFC after his two and half years of service, I suspect Anderson did not adapt well. In any case, he certainly is paying back the Pentagon hucksters.

"I got a whole load of those 'postage free' advertising cards used by the recruiting branch of each service. I got all I could from every source I could—post offices, recruiting stations, stores. Then some friends and I began filling them out, using the names of other fascist bastards as potential recruits, like local hawk politicians, draft supporters, ROTC kids at school, local cops, anyone who was a bullying authority figure. We mailed them all in, staggering the mailings and the mailed-from locations."

Anderson explained his scam brought several results, including a drain on the military recruiting budget for postage costs, telephone calls and recruiters' time. It also hassled the establishment marks who had to put up with all the calls and contacts from the military which thought they were legitimate inquires.

Personally, I deplore this sort of unpatriotic behavior. The military—love it or leave it, I say!

Our nation's recall of the military conscription system brought out a lot of anti-draft scams. However, one trick uses the recruitment system for a rather elaborate campaign to defeat your mark's reputation if that mark is the military.

Unionization of the armed forces is a topic that tarnishes the brasshats, making it an ideal red herring to sucker the lifers and others who take it all so seriously. Former U.S. Navy vet, CPO Otis Crool, says that one of his favorites was to create leaflets using official paper and mimeo machines.

He explains, "I'd run up these really radical leaflets exhorting my fellow Navy cannonfodder to campaign for unionization of the armed forces. I'd include totally unreasonable demands that made the wobblies look like a bunch of capitalists.

"The fun came when I'd sign these leaflets with the name of my mark—usually an officer or senior

CPO who was a dedicated asshole. I'd use his name, rank, unit, then include his home address and telephone. Naturally, I urged 'fellow comrade worker-soldiers' to contact him personally."

Neighbors

If you've taken the twist to "Hate Thy Neighbor" for good reason, here's a dynamite idea sent in by Neil Burger. Neil says to collect all the empty bottles you can which carry labels of DANGEROUS, EX-PLOSIVES, DRUGS, and so on. Add to this empty dynamite cartons from a construction site. Or, if you want to be even more low profile so as not to get the actual thing, go to an art shop, get stencils and spray paint your own box and bottle labels.

Put all these dangerous things in and around your neighbor's garbage can after he has put his own stuff out at curbside. Do this for several weeks. The civic-minded sanitary engineers will probably report your "crackpot" neighbor to the police. If they haven't, as a solid citizen, you should . . . from a pay telephone.

If you can't blast them out, how about a frame? This variation could be subtitled "The Feds," according to A. J. Waterman, an old correspondent who suggested it. He says you send out a well-dressed, deadpan, square-looking "FBI agent" to make obvious inquiries about a "gang of dangerous subversive terrorists." Guess where these subver-sives live? Right . . . your mark's address. Your "agent" should show the neighbors some blurry photos taken of people on that street, hinting they are terrorists. Of course, the photos will be of the mark, his or her friends and/or family, and, for sure, the mark's car.

Oil Companies

A chuckle-humored Georgia reader sent his favorite oil company a delightfully devised letter, which he was willing to share with us. Dan Streetman says of his letter, "I can only gleefully imagine the havoc and expense visited upon the accounting department when this letter is handed down from the top." Here is his letter.

Dear *(Chairman of the Board):*

This is the tenth anniversary of my association with _____ Oil, and I would like to take this opportunity to thank you personally for your corporation's unflagging generosity.

It started, I suppose, with my credit application which was promptly denied for reasons I've long since forgotten. Then, strangely enough, a charge card from your company bearing my name followed shortly thereafter.

I began to use the new card routinely, assuming your credit department had simply made an error in rejecting my application. I might add I used the card exclusively as I had no other gas and oil card. Two, three, four months passed; then one day it occurred to me that I had received no bill. Not one. Though I kept few receipts I calculated my charges to be well over a hundred dollars at the time. As the expiration date stamped on the card approached I was certain the computer accounting error would be revealed, a mammoth bill would be sent, and no replacement card issued.

The years have clipped by now, as I've said, ten in all, and as regular as the seasons a colorful new plastic card arrives just in time to replace the old one; but never an invoice.

As gasoline prices have risen so drastically in the last couple of years I have been forced to spread your generosity by sharing my credit privileges with my friends who have found their budgets shorted by ever rising fuel costs.

This morning I had a new set of your finest line tires installed on my car. This afternoon for his birthday I am giving my friend Bob a tune-up and a brake job at another of your many, many stations. He, too, sends best wishes for your continued success. After all these years I have grown confident that my name and number are locked, eternally silent, in a minuscule electrical impulse somewhere in some computer's faulty diode, or transistor, or senile memory bank.

Or, it may simply be that I have a secret friend or philosophical admirer in your company itself— someone who is helping me, unbeknownst to me. I wonder how many other folks are being "helped" this way and have chosen not to write you?

Unable to repay you now even if I were billed, I can only send you this note of teeming thanks.

Sincerely,

A Very Satisfied Customer

Don't you just love that dash of paranoia-producer sprinkled in at the end of the next to last paragraph? Actually, with variation and modification this letter can be used for any large credit card operation or for most utility companies. A little imagination plus some adaptation will give you a custom letter to pay back some corporate tormentor, too.

Party

Credit and a tip of the hat to Mike Cooch for this one. It seems you want to get back at someone who holds a lot of parties. There are myriad reasons. In any case, if your hated hosts take the crowd out for a late dinner, if they adjourn to the pool, or leave the house for whatever reason, it's always funny to change the entire lock in their door.

According to Mike, this works well if it is a small apartment with only one door. It doesn't take very long to do this, either.

A much more crude substitute was suggested by David George of Holmestreet, Alaska, who wrote, "You just get all of the jerks inside an apartment, then screw a heavy-duty hasp and padlock on the outside. If you really want to let them stew, cut the phone lines, too. It's funnier than hell."

While you're at it, why not cut the electric power, and the water, too?

Politicians

You can build a photographic frame around the candidate of your dischoice. Suppose one of these slugs displeases you more than the others, for any number of valid reasons. You need some scuzzy friends to pull this one off. You wear a t-shirt with a militant slogan at extreme odds with the politician, e.g. POLITICIANS ARE INEVITABLY IDIOTS. But, you have it disguised under something, like a book bag or by holding a newspaper in front of yourself. Your odd friends cluster behind the politician.

This works best at campaign time when there are a lot of cameras around. You come up to the politico/mark with your hand extended for the usual shake. Your partners move into position—clustered around the two of you. As you and the mark shake hands this is what will appear in the photo:

- You reveal your messaged t-shirt.
- One of your pals behind the mark gives the raised/clenched fist salute.
- Several of your pals hug and pretend to french kiss each other, as in a gaggle of guys.
- Another of your pals exposes himself.
- Another produces a bottle in a brown bag.
- And, so on. . . .

125

If your photos turn out you have that candidate by his or her photogenic short hairs.

Not everyone was thrilled by the 1980 Presidential campaign facade. A few folks expressed supreme displeasure about the direct mail advertising solicitations disguised as public opinion polls. One contributor elected to do something about these unsought postal intruders.

"When I received a request to contribute to Ronald Reagan's 'victory' campaign I decided not to get indignant about that senile old fraud," Ralph Meyers reports.

"I went to a friend who collects really disgusting porno and borrowed some especially ripe and graphic specimens. I stuffed each of Mr. Reagan's prepaid business-reply envelopes with the gross porno. The stuff really was explicit and foul . . . homosexuals, women with animals, kiddie porn . . . stuff like that.

"I regard politicians as pornographic, especially Reagan and Carter, and since they sent me their unsolicited porno, I was free to do the same."

Porno

Yes, porno theaters can cause problems in a neighborhood simply because of some of the pathetic slimes who are drawn there like slugs to a wet garden. Or, you can be ripped off by a porno theater that promises you a loop done by Brooke Shields in her early years, showing her wrestling naked with, well, you fill in your favorite fantasy. But, it's merely a raunchy lookalike. Sigh. You're out $10.

How to get even?

Dress up like some pimpy businessperson, slick back your hair, then buy a ticket and go into the theater. Once inside, start handing out free passes you had printed just for this occasion.

The passes are a special invitation to see a commercially produced snuff film, with a real on-camera homicide. If you want to go the trouble and expense, print a little brochure with obscene photos and maybe a composite showing some sexual and/or violent action. You can probably get pictures of this garbage from militant feminist groups who want to publicize the degradation of obscene films. Put the address of the porno theater (your mark) on the brochure along with a time and date. Work quickly and get out of there as soon as possible.

As an additional fun thing, on the day of the "showing," be certain to get these same passes and brochure to local media people, clergy, feminist groups, local redneck politicans, police, etc.

Just suppose, for the sake of argument, that some fat jackass of a District Attorney or shyster lawyer for some blue-nosed Citizens for Decent Literature group wins one of their censorship cases. These lowlifes are the bookburners who piously demand that all of us follow their stupidly squalid moral misvalues. Here's how Emmett Hilliard got even when they closed down his book store in Gipsy, Missouri because a copy of SPORTS ILLUSTRATED had a picture on its cover of a lady in a bikini.

"I found the most graphic and active swingers' magazine I could. Then, I searched up in the city for the foulest and most perverted sexual magazines published. And, in each, I placed a small display advertisement for the leader of the local Bible bangers who closed me down."

His ad read:

FREE

TALK YOUR DIRTIEST FOR ONE MINUTE

Call this number and say the dirtiest most perverted things you can think of . . . my friend and I will outdo you. Cum again? We hope so.
Ring our dingy!!!

Name . . . Home Telephone Number

According to Hilliard, every sewer mouth from Fairlawn to Niwot, from Butler to Helsinki lathed the ears of the mark, his wife and hs daughter until he finally had to have his telephone number changed . . . several times.

"The best part is that it took three months from when he did me dirty until I got back, because of publication lag and all that. It was great. I will hit him again," says Hilliard.

This next trick will work well if your mark is a spoiled brat or bratess who has not yet been cut loose from the family apron. Get a rubber stamp made that says something tacky like YEE SEXY LEATHER SHOPPE, or S & M LEATHERETTES, or something else that implies kinky, gay sex involving leather, freakos, S & M, etc. Apply the imprint to a cheapie type manila mailing envelope with a metal clasp on it. Fill this envelope with gay magazines, explicit brochures, S & M propaganda, etc. Then, get a lady with nice handwriting to write a note on cutesy pink paper. The note should be addressed to your mark personally and say something like, "Bunny gave us your home address, sweetcakes. He/she said you'd enjoy dreaming about our next gay ball if you had these to look at first while you fantasize about doing it with us. Keep cumming back to our parties. Love, Brucie."

Don't glue this envelope shut. Simply seal it. Then, address it to your mark and send it to his home address. Hopefully, it will create some wildly *loco parentis*.

Posters

Here's one that John Bowen calls his "Tribute to Dallas." If you have an incumbent President you don't like, run off a few of the "(NAME OF PRESIDENT): WANTED FOR TREASON" posters of the type that were used in Dallas the week before President Kennedy was murdered there by some determined assassins. They used JFK's name as the traitor. Your kicker is that you put your mark's name in small type as sponsor of the poster, then list some affiliation, e.g., the Klan, the Birchers, the Nazis, the U.S. Labor Party, etc., under his name. Obviously, this can be used at most any level of politics.

There are also political endorsement modifications available on this one. Think of all the fun you can have with gay rights groups, pro-life, or pro-abortion people who could have their "names" listed on the posters you're having printed.

Railroads

Generally, railroads are good folks. Why our country doesn't utilize and depend upon rail transportation like European and Asian nations has always puzzled me. Perhaps the airline and auto industries have too much lobby muscle. But, sometimes people who work for the railways screw up. When they do, L.T., our faithful correspondent from Mark Twain land, has a splendid way to derail them.

L.T. explains that every railroad car has a square plate with blue, red, white and black lines on it. When the cars pass by a computer-fed sensor, the rail company keeps track of their rolling stock and their destinations, using these colors which are read by the sensor.

Waving a guilty-colored can of spray paint, L.T. reveals, "If you paint over these lines, the rail people and their flawless computer are lost for awhile. You know how costly down time can be . . . for stock and computers."

He adds that the old fashioned lead base paint works excellently, and he's not certain if the new latex paints are as effective.

Religion

This one's pretty rough and if you have a streak of old fashioned religion in you, perhaps you'd best skip this section. The Rev. Sam Clayton Neucomber split with traditional religion some years ago and now fights the IRS and other establishment evils from his own parish in Arizona.

He says, "It's not enough to merely corrupt the mark's religious beliefs or to start rumors about him or her in the church. You have to do more, especially if your mark is a church or a movement."

If your mark is a house of worship or the worldly master of that house, e.g., the religious person in charge, the good Rev. Neucomber has some interesting ideas.

"It's not nearly enough just to insult or mock a religious mark," says Rev. Neucomber. "You must go beyond the mere passion of punks or vandals. To really flip out your mark you must create a scene that leaves no doubt the religious shrine or church or whatever was broken into for the express purpose of holding a Black Mass, for example.

"The mark will call out to God, asking what manner of devil or demented heathen would desecrate His house of worship in such a way. Here's where imagination comes in well."

Some of Rev. Neucomber's suggestions for evidence of a Black Mass include:

• Leave animal blood, unless you can get human blood in quantity, on marble areas or splashed over the altar.

• Leave an especially ghoulish animal sacrifice there too.

• If there is a table cloth there, perhaps for communion services, you can adorn it with occult symbols and bestial graffiti.

• Scatter photos around which show naked women blindfolded, bound and gagged. Make sure some of the photos show the women in sexually open and totally vulnerable positions. Child porn would work here, too.

• Mutilate some of these photos, marking them with blood and symbolically destroying genital areas.

• Leave used condoms around—some filled with semen, others with blood.

• Use some of the mark's fine chalices and leave a few half filled with urine. Pour blood in a couple and be sure at least one has semen in it.

Phew . . . if you're still with us, did you ever work with a religious hot dog, the type who overtries to convert everyone else in the place? Dingo L. Stuart had to put up with one of these yo yo's during his tour of duty working in a large factory. Tiring of the Bible banger's shrieks and tirades, Stuart called on his pal, who worked in a print shop.

Together, they came up with sophisticated looking ecclesiastical stationery on which they printed CERTIFICATE OF EXORCISM in an old fashioned churchy-appearing type style. The document stated, "In a Secret Ceremony witnessed by (name all sorts of angels, martyrs, deceased heroes, etc.) the Reverend (Use name of some other mark) did hereby and forever expel and exorcize the unclean spirits from the body and soul of (Name your main mark here), releasing him from the torments of everlasting hell and damnation. (Name of main mark)'s soul will now ascend to His Paradise."

Feel free to edit or rewrite that as you wish, customizing it for your mark. Stuart says to include with this statement an itemized fee schedule for the Exorcism, including the cleric's fee, costs for candles, incense, bottled blood, vestments which had to be burned, a sacrificial calf or goat—use your imagination. Total it, then send the entire thing to the mark's supervisor, along with a bogus cover letter on the same letterhead asking the employer's help in dunning the employee who has not paid for the exorcism.

As a possible alternative plan, you could simply send a letter on that letterhead to the supervisor, from the Reverend, saying that the main mark, the religious nut employee, had suggested his name (the employer or supervisor) as being in need of salvation, or even an exorcism, too. Include a copy of that exorcism statement mentioned earlier.

Roadkill

There are always rednecks who love to destroy animals who venture out on our interventionist highways. I remember almost dismembering some illiterate jackass who was driving an UPS truck down the lane to my old home fortress a few months back. He was proud that he'd run over a blacksnake on my lane. He told me so. I was not thrilled and told him that that specific snake kept little varmints out of my garden. His sloped brow sunk lower, then he told me that he read in the *National Enquirer* that blacksnakes and rattlesnakes were mating, causing a new breed of poisonous snake. I told him I wished his parents had heard of birth control, but probably not so much as they did now, like every time they saw him. He took a swing at me five minutes later, when what I said sunk through the bone. He later threatened to sue me for the damages he then picked up. Later, calling him at home, I told him he'd better watch out for his mailbox as I had friends in Synanon who trained rattlesnakes.

Whatever, I researched his route and talked to people who lived along it. I learned he would swerve to scare dogs playing along the road. One old soul told me that this UPS driver seemed to have a thing for running over animals on purpose.

Thanks to some help from a friend of a friend of a friend at the SPCA, I found a dog that had been freshly killed by a passing car. I had that friend claim the carcass and get it to me. I armed it with some low grade explosives, wired it with a very simple pressure detonator that you can duplicate by reading a specific military demolition manual, then laid it along the route taken by my UPS mark.

Sure enough, numbnuts tried to squash the already dead dog one more time. The ordnance did its thing and his company vehicle was minus one tire, had another one flattened, there was minor structural damage, while our driver was a total nervous wreck. It took him one week to get physically together and three more weeks before he could get into another truck. The best is that UPS and his union disciplined him for reckless operation.

Rubbers

Here's a quickie that can annoy your mark, if you have easy access to his boots, overshoes or rubbers on a winter or rainy day. If you know when he or she is going to be putting them on, pour some slow drying glue into the footwear a bit before they go on the mark's shoes. Spread the stuff around so it bonds well.

Sources

Neil Pendleton says that the fabulous Yellow Pages of the Bell Telephone Directory inspire his dirty tricks. "Oh yes, if I spend a half an hour drifting through the 'yellow pages' with my mind set on Nasty, I can get all sorty sorts of inventive ideas."

Let your mind do the walking and your imagination do the wandering. . . .

J. C. WHITNEY & CO., P.O. Box 8410, Chicago, IL 60680 is the national center for anything and everything automotive. Several auto tricksters buy their nasty accessories and supplies from Whitney because they have it all.

Another excellent shopping place for our ilk is SARGENT SOWELL, INC., a huge mail order house out of Grand Prairie, TX 75050. They go by the trade name SA-SO, and stock a trickster's wealth of delight. Their enormous catalog is a wishbook for the suburban prankster and his urban guerilla friend. The rural commando will find it a dream, too. SA-SO sells everything and anything in the world a muncipality or its agencies would ever use, e.g., roadsigns, traffic signs and signals, road markers, office supplies, security devices, police equipment,

140

industrial chemicals, etc. They sell all sorts of things to give you the cover trappings of being an establishment/government worker or official, including identification systems. They sell the supplies that enable you to pull off any sort of scam using some municipal service as your cover or excuse or mark. In short, given access to the SA-SO catalog and enough money you can masquerade as a municipality. How's that for the keys to the candy store?

A real treatful catalog comes from THE BROOK-STONE COMPANY in Peterborough, NH 03458. They advertise hard to find tools, unusual devices and "other fine things." It's that last line which should interest you, i.e., you can get most of the glues, synthetic oils and compounds mentioned in my books from them. For example, they sell both speed-setting and slow drying glues. One glue will grab 200 psi strength in only 30 minutes and human holding power in just five. They also sell a glue which gives you 36 hours to cure your mark, so to speak. They sell a midget grease gun that's perfect for surreptitious amusement. They sell a tough, single component metal paste that is not just another filler compound. This is the real thing and it works just great. They sell a totally indestructible hasp/case/padlock combination that defies torches and saws . . . perfect for locking in that special someone or something which doesn't want or need to be locked in.

Or, they sell adhesive-backed magnetic tape; glass and ceramic patch that really does work like a miracle; instant aerosol Urethane foam; a portable high altitude tree pruner that lets you make quick, sharp cuts 30 feet or more above you; a tough

Tantalum carbide engraver that will cut almost any substance; Weldbond—the one "space age" adhesive that really does work, unlike all the bullshit ones advertised on TV.

An excellent book to help you do your pre-strike intelligence gathering and analysis is *The Muckraker's Manual,* written by someone named M. Harry. This useful and inexpensive reference book is available from LOOMPANICS UNLIMITED, P.O. Box 1197, Port Townsend, WA 98368. Get a copy of their valuable catalog, too; it's very useful. For example, Loompanics has books which tell you all about, how to use and where to find mail drops, remailing services, false IDs, aliases, and all the other services so vital to a serious trickster. The Loompanics catalog is quite easily the most complete bibliography imaginable for this book of mine.

If you're under 40, or were never a kid, this source won't mean as much to you. Johnson-Smith now sells novelties and advertises itself as "The Funhouse." Back when I was a kid, Johnson-Smith was the class clown's dreamworld, a mail order catalog that you had to hide from your folks. Mere possession of this catalog in school meant being sent home. Johnson-Smith openly sold itching powder, sneezing powder, cigarette loads, burn-their-mouth candy, whoppee cushions, joy buzzers, and all that other good stuff a fledgling trickster used in his operations.

I saw their current catalog and I guess like the rest of us, Johnson-Smith had to grow up and join the '80s. Sigh. Even their address seems an ironic shame, 35075 Automation Dr., Mt. Clemens, MI 48043. Automation Drive? Good Lord!

But, there are still some old goodies in there and a few new ones, like disguise masks, realistic looking fake snakes (the use of which I can vouch for), foul-tasting chewing gum, and so forth. Although their tricks are now fairly tame, I am including Johnson-Smith for both nostalgic and possible resource use.

Another valuable source of manuals on mayhem is Paladin Press, P.O. Box 1307, Boulder, CO 80306, publisher of this tome. Send $1 for their titillating catalog.

Sweethearts

Did you ever notice those tabloids and semi-skin flicks that run classified ads headlined "Foreign Girls Looking For American Husbands." One young lady learned about that after her married lover ditched her because *she* made the stupid mistake of getting pregnant by him. Instead of moping, she had the good sense to get even with the subhuman slimeball. Here's how.

"I sent off a response to one of those ads, written as if a hot to go, but sincere, guy who wanted both marriage and action would write it," she told me. "I heard enough of that kind of BS from that (expletive deleted) who burned me."

What happens is that the foreign recipient will get the hot letter and she will go directly to the mark. The foreign stamp on the envelope and lady's handwriting will cause great curiosity on the part of the mark's wife. She might say, "Hmmm, we don't know anyone in the Philippines . . . do WE?"

The next sound you hear is an envelope being opened.

The next idea is a bit different. It started when the girl slapped Frank Fogge, gave him back his picture and told him to get lost. She had been won over by a kid with more money and status on the football team. She said she'd carry The New Sweetie's picture with her forever. She told Frank this new love was inscribed on her soul.

Fogge was no dummy, and he didn't mope around either. He got even. He gave her another picture to think about.

Using a standard billing form available from any stationery department, Fogge prepared a bogus invoice from "Sammy's Tattoo Parlor," complete with address and a catchy business motto. He got the business logo done by instant lettering, an inexpensive commercial process, then filled in the invoice information by hand. He also got a rubber stamp that spelled OVERDUE in big letters, and put a huge red stamping of this on the invoice.

Finally, he wrote a cover letter from "Sammy," explaining to the ex-girlfriend's parents that their daughter had gotten "a tasteful facial tattoo," but, that she was now upset after a few days and was refusing to pay for it. He wrote that it would make a huge scar if it were removed, and that he just wanted to be paid. He noted, "She is your problem now, but I want my money."

On the other hand, if your mark is a newlywed, or one of those Pat Boone squares, this trick is quite nice. Your printer sets up and prints a "Preferred Customer Credit Voucher" sales gimmick. The rest of the copy informs the holder that he will get a $10 credit toward a "full body massage with complete fulfillment by our . . ." you can use your prurient imagination to fill in the nubile delights of the maiden whose hands, mouth and other goodies will delightfully satisfy the customer.

You send this card to the mark's business address in hopes his secretary will open it. Or, if your mark doesn't have a secretary, send it home. Make it personal and put perfume on it. If his blue-turning, red hot wife doesn't open it, she surely as hell will demand he does, in front of her. Do you note a different type of massage or even message coming up?

A really nasty friend gave me this one. This chap is so bad he has plastered his car bumper with NUKE THE WHALES stickers, while his favorite adult toy to tinker with is a submachine gun. He's a good beer drinker and has a very nasty turn of mind. I guess that's why we're friends.

Anyway, it seems a friend of my friend got the shaft from his former girl friend who tossed him over for a richer man who was able to entertain her on a champagne budget. He wanted to get back at the snooty bitch. Happily, her father was a real racist redneck, which made it easier.

His scam went like this. Our young man got a black friend who has mastered a real Stepin Fetchit approach to the Negro dialect. The black buddy called the girl's home telephone at some ungodly hour of the early morning, knowing full well the young woman lived in her own apartment elsewhere in the city. When the sleepy parent answered, the buddy launched into his hip-black monologue, saying that Ellen was supposed to come back to his pad to pick up some personal effects she had left there last night.

According to my pal, this trick will provoke the racist, over-protective father into a state of cardiac paranoia. When it was first tried by my friend, he said it took the father 20 minutes to dress and drive across the city to rescue "his little girl" from the subhuman clutches of her imaginary Black stud. Watching the fun from a nearby room, my friend reported a terrible argument with much shouting and ranting. This wakened the neighbors, creating more fuss and furor. Eventually, the police had to be called. It was great sport, according to my friend. It sounds it to me, too.

Then, there is the story of Young Sam, who dated a coed who treated him like a visiting monk. In the meantime, she milked his jealousy by flirting with all sorts of other guys at parties. When they were alone, she kept her clothes on tighter than a professional virgin. When Sam learned her parents were coming to visit he had a plan. He acquired some suspiciously stained men's underwear of the sexy type. He made little typed plaques with the autographs of some campus studs, e.g., Black football players, etc., plus inscriptions like "To _____ , for a wild evening of laughter, love and turn-ons," or, "Wow, _____ , I told you a threesome was more fun . . . love, _____ ."

While sweet young thing was out to meet her parents Sam snuck into her apartment and mounted the trophies on the wall of her bedroom. He left the rest to the imagination of her parents.

You've heard of the pregnant pause? You want to break up with your two-timing lady? Daniel Jacson has the answer. He says you should take this lady out for a fashionable meal in a very posh restaurant. Or, if you live in a small town, take her to the place where all the old gossips chow down. Whatever, after ordering the most expensive stuff on the menu, about the time the little snacks and talk food are served, stand bold-upright, look at her, then scream, "PREGNANT? Pregnant, my ass! You never did that with ME!!"

Then, you slam down your napkin and stride quickly out of the place. She has to pay for both meals *and* has some explaining to do.

Not everyone is like that. There's a nice young lady who used to call herself Becky Buckeye. But, with the coming of Born Again Reagan Power, she changed her name to Becky Beaver. I'm not even going to attempt any thoughts about all that. As you'll agree, her diabolical suggestion is all the bonefides she needs in our movement.

Becky relates that a friend of hers had some man problems in that he wouldn't limit his personal charms to her.

Becky says, "She planted a birth control pill box with a few days punched and the rest missed. Now, some people might not start counting days. But, this guy would begin to mark off a mental calendar."

For those of you who are not physio-chemically inclined, Becky explains that the mark will think his lady friend was not taking her pill each day, which can easily lead to one becoming of the pregnant persuasion if other variables are also present. The point is to panic the man into thinking he is soon to become an involuntary parent.

Becky's friend says this causes all sorts of anxieties, paranoia, personality quirks and expression of true feelings. The latter is especially important. Becky also adds that if the mark doesn't have a steady woman this is far less effective as a trick on him.

Here's one Wilbur Aaron was itching to share with like-minded readers. Seems a snotty little bitch was patronizing and nasty to Wilbur Aaron's best friend when she told him their romance was over right then and there. She said coldly, "I'm itching to meet someone with more class and money. You're nothing but a weed in my social garden."

With that, she signed on as a habitué of the local singles bar meat markets in hopes of meeting true love and lust. Instead of hoping she'd meet Mr. Goodbar, Wilbur's friend thought about what she'd told him. He came up with an extremely clever use of poison ivy.

"Although it was a month or so after she tossed him out for no good reason other than her own ego, he still had a key to her place that she'd forgotten about. Thus, he had easy acces to the leotard she wore to her dance class," Wilbur reports.

The lacerated ex-lover liberally smeared the groin and chest areas inside of the leotard with crushed poison ivy. Later that day, the exertion in her dance class opened up her pores and she soon had a splendid outbreak of the virulent rash in those most sensitive areas.

"As she washed the leotard after every class she never associated it with that mysterious rash that popped up two days later. It was a dilly," Wilbur adds.

Supermarkets

In addition to switching labels on food cans, described elsewhere in this work, one of my disciples suggests buying the new pump bottles of such things as furniture and car polish, taking them home, then replacing the original contents with harmful acids and corrosive contents. Next, smuggle them back into the store, or directly into your mark's home if possible, depending on who or what your mark is. Hee Hee, watch the mark really get red and raw hands from the old chores . . . not to mention the old redass!!

Swimming Pools

John Lutz, a libation specialist, made a delightful discovery while shopping for something actively stronger than those comedic "I DON'T SWIM IN YOUR TOILET, SO PLEASE DON'T PEE IN MY POOL" posters that do so little. He learned that a chemical substance sold by the trade name of Aquatect makes a positively great additive to your swimming pool water.

"It is odorless and colorless and cannot be detected in the pool, until a swimmer pees, then the chemical reacts with the urine and creates a bright red stain around the culprit," Lutz explains.

Toilets

Perhaps you are unhappy with some religious sect or establishment church. Find an especially disgusting toilet which is filled-to-overflowing unflushable, and thus churning with stomach-turning contents and odor. You will place neatly printed stick-on labels on the stall door. Each plaque reads:

DO NOT FLUSH
A (Name of Religion) BAPTISMAL FONT

It is great to do this in a hotel just as a group of visiting religious freaks from that particular persuasion are checking in for a convention. A friend of mine did this because of truly evil things the Mormon Church did to his wife. He printed his cards ending in "A MORMON BAPTISMAL FONT." He reports that when the Latter Day Saints came marching into the hotel and saw the stickers, they threatened the management with the wrath of Joseph Smith and His sidekick, God.

As an extra touch, my friend said he used a couple pens to scribble doodles and phone numbers on the stickers, added a few graffiti, wore down the edges, then smudged them . . . all to make the stickers appear that they'd been there for awhile. This would, of course, indicate the tacit approval of hotel employees and management. It added to the impact a great deal, he said.

Utility Companies

Stop reading. Put this book down and think for a moment about the effect on your immediate life there at home if you were suddenly denied water or electricity. Who controls our electric power and our water supplies? Mostly, a monopoly known as a public utility controls these creature comforts. That fact makes stunts involving these utility companies work mightily to your advantage.

Several years ago, a nasty, nosey neighbor was hassling, prying and spying on a very nice person who read my first book and wrote to me about all this. After waiting awhile to avert suspicion, this reader visited the nasty neighbor's mailbox while that evil person was at work. Only the water company bill, and nothing else, was removed. At this point, the nasty neighbor became the mark.

This went on for several months. The dunning notices were also stolen. A cancellation of service notice was removed. A final notice was taken out. Then, one day, a water company crew arrived to shut off the mark's water. It took several dry days to straighten out the entire situation. This stunt didn't cure the neighbor's nasty habits, but it gave the reader a sense of getting back.

I should add that some folks who work for the U.S. Postal Monopoly regard "mail tampering" as a very serious federal offense. Be careful.

Although it's only a temporary inconvenience you can easily shut off your mark's electricity or water at the meter or the main circuit breaker, then use a heavy padlock to bar easy access to opening the service again. According to several contributors this is a proven winner and works very well in smaller apartment complexes and condominium units.

A more sophisticated bit of amusement is making your mark late for work or school by shutting down the power for an hour or so in the dead of night, then turning it back on again. Unless the mark has a windup or digital clock, the alarm will go off when programmed on the mechanism. His or her problem is that the actual time will be an hour or so later, because of your manipulation of the main power circuit. Being late for work and not knowing it until he or she gets there, then not knowing why, is a great way for your mark to start off his or her day.

If you're interested in a more subtle and maddening method of the Haydukian Water Torture for your mark(s), read away. This one makes your mark a person, the water company, or both. The idea here is to visit the main valve of your mark's water meter every couple of days. Shut down the pressure by a half to a full turn every few days. The mark's entire household will go nuts trying to figure out why the water pressure is steadily dropping all week. Then, jack it all the way back again for a day or so. OK, now cut it way down. Put it halfway up. Cut it to almost a trickle. Go for full power. Then, cut it again. By this time the mark will have the water company out. If you have quick enough access to the valve you can restore it to normal before the water company employee gets to the meter. When the employee leaves, start again. Eventually, they will dig up the yard and check the pipes. This one has been a tried and proved winner for several people.

Vending Machines

A reader named Joe Morris has a profitable sense of humor about being ripped off by a vending machine. Joe says that so many people get ripped off so often that it's hard to find an innocent machine anymore. Here's his idea.

"I don't want to damage the machine, just the reputation of its owner. And, I want to get back my money and a little interest in return.

"All you need is a big wad of cotton, like the kind that comes in a roll at the drug store. Wrap a wire around it and stuff it up the coin return shaft in the machine, until the wire is just above the opening and can't be seen. The next day, come back, pull out your wire and receive a refund of the fullest kind."

Joe says this works only on the machines that don't have covers over the coin returns. He says it works like a charm on machines which drop the change right into the same tray as the product. But, clog just the coin shaft, not the product shaft. Otherwise . . . zero.

Weapons

According to L.T. from Mark Twain Land, a crossbow is a splendid weapon to use for creative revenge. My Twainian friend notes the crossbow may be used for silent attacks on domestic ar:mals, breaking windows, putting holes in buildings or vehicles, or scaring the excrement out of a mark via a near miss. In some localities, crossbows are illegal, but then, so is marijuana.

There are lesser weapons. Thomas Bicipieu had an uncaring neighbor who allowed his large and uncivilized dogs to roam all over Thomas's property, leaving their large, unsightly and smelly calling cards all over the lawn, flowers, and garden. After several gentle, neighborly complaints, followed by a rather stiff telephone call, Thomas noticed no lessening of the doggie dung.

"I'll fight fire with spray, so to speak," he vowed.

With that, he took an empty spray bottle of the type used to squirt anticongestant up one's nose as in those horrible TV commercials. He made the opening a bit larger so it could be emptied faster. He filled it with fresh urine after a long, hard night of drinking beer and eating hard-boiled eggs.

Thomas began to make sneak attacks on his neighbor's automobile, spraying load after load into the car's interior as he passed by several times while walking his own leashed and trained dog. Thomas reports that in summer's heat, the stench of stale urine does wonders for the interior of a car . . . not to mention the fringe benefit of seat stains.

According to Mr. Bicipieu, this same weapon may be used to pay back merchants who have wronged you—especially clothing, food or furniture people. If you dare not walk into the store itself, you can always discharge a much larger vessel—say a quart or half gallon sized container—into the air conditioner intake.

Dispense properly, urine is wonderful stuff.

Women's Stores

This one works wonderfully well at those old line stores where people like your mother or a proper aunt buy their fancy clothes. You mount a small TV camera-like box on one of the top corners of the dressing cubicle where ladies try on their prospective purchases. Tape a small printed sign under the box, noting, "For Private Security Purposes Only, Do Not Be Alarmed." Sign the card with name of the store manager. Your printer made these signs for you.

If you wish to be even more ballsy, add the following message, too. "Mature security personnel destroy all photographs immediately if there is no evidence of retail theft." According to one field report this last sign blushed up a storm that almost ended in a lawsuit against the store.

Why such a rotten trick? In an earlier case of mistaken identity, store security personnel had challenged a totally innocent woman, accusing her of being a shoplifter. They weren't going to let her go, up to and including the store manager, until she mentioned she was dating a local activist attorney—which was a bit of an exaggeration, because she knew him only as a social acquaintence.

Later, this young lady proceeded with the scam outlined above . . . much more fun than a real lawsuit. And, as she points out, when your settlement is outstanding laughter, you don't have to share an outrageous sum of it with some lawyer.